5th edition

International
English

A guide to the varieties
of Standard English

Peter Trudgill

& Jean Hannah

Routledge
Taylor & Francis Group

LONDON AND NEW YORK

First edition published in Great Britain in 1982 by Edward Arnold
This fifth edition published 2008 by Hodder Education

Published 2013 by Routledge
2 Park Square, Milton Park, Abingdon, Oxon OX14 4RN
711 Third Avenue, New York, NY, 10017, USA

Routledge is an imprint of the Taylor & Francis Group, an informa business

The advice and information in this book are believed to be true and
accurate at the date of going to press, but neither the authors nor the publisher
can accept any legal responsibility or liability for any errors or omissions.

British Library Cataloguing in Publication Data
A catalogue record for this title is available from the British Library

Library of Congress Cataloging-in-Publication Data
A catalog record of this book is available from the Library of Congress

ISBN 13: 978-0-340-97161-1 (pbk)

Typeset by MPS Limited

5th edition

International

English

For Mum, Dad and Mom

Contents

Note to the Fifth Edition   *ix*
Acknowledgements   *xi*
Symbols   *xiii*

1   Standard English in the world   1
    1.1. Models of English   4
    1.2. The spread of English   8
    1.3. The nature of native overseas Englishes   11

2   English, Australasian, South African and Welsh English   15
    2.1. The RP accent   15
    2.2. Australian, New Zealand and South African English   21
    2.3. Welsh English   36

3   The pronunciation of North American English   41
    3.1. North American English vowels   41
    3.2. North American English consonants   45
    3.3. Regional variation in United States English   45
    3.4. The pronunciation of Canadian English   53
    3.5. Non-systematic differences between North
          American English and English English pronunciation   55
    3.6. Stress differences   56
    3.7. Further differences between American English and
          Canadian English pronunciation   58

4   English and North American English: grammatical,
    orthographical and lexical differences   59
    4.1. Grammatical differences   59
    4.2. Spelling and punctuation differences   83
    4.3. Vocabulary differences   87

5   Scottish and Irish English   95
    5.1. Scottish English   95
    5.2. English in Ireland   103

6   West Indian English and English-based creoles   109
     6.1. English-based pidgins   109
     6.2. English-based creoles   111
     6.3. Decreolization   112
     6.4. Post-creoles and mesolectal varieties   114
     6.5. West Indian Standard English   116
     6.6. English-based creoloids   118

7   Lesser-known Englishes   119

8   Second language varieties of English   127
     8.1. West African English   128
     8.2. East African English   132
     8.3. Indian English   133
     8.4. Singaporean English   139
     8.5. English in the Philippines   142

Glossary   *145*
Selected references and further reading   *149*
Index   *153*

Note to the Fifth Edition

Encouraged by our publishers to act on the observation that 'things are happening' in the English-speaking world, we have decided that the time is ripe for another edition of our book. The English language itself is changing, as all languages do – one of the features of this new edition is a discussion of the extent to which lexical 'Americanisms' have now found their way into British and other Englishes. And the sociolinguistic situations in which English is spoken have also altered – it made sense to talk about the vestigial prestige associated with the RP accent in Australia in 1982, but it makes much less sense now. We have also expanded the accompanying audio material – available on the website – by adding a recording of the very interesting English of Singapore – an originally second-language variety of the language which is now acquiring native speakers. And we have also taken note of the growing discussion around the world about which varieties of English should be used as models for the teaching of English as a second and foreign language. However, since a major practical aim of this book is to familiarise readers with as many varieties of English as possible with a view to improving comprehension, we have not argued here in favour of any particular model or models.

One of us is British and the other American, so we have always had ready access to information about the English of these two countries. Aware of our relative lack of immediate experience of the English of the other native English-speaking regions of the world, we have also over the years managed to travel to Canada, Ireland, Australia, New Zealand and the Caribbean in order to investigate for ourselves the varieties of English spoken in these places. At the time of writing, of the major varieties of mother-tongue English around the world, only our section on South African English is not based on our own observations. We have also carried out research in the Bahamas and Bermuda (see Chapter 6). The sections on Indian and Singaporean English are also based on research *in situ*.

The subject of this book continues to be Standard English, as it is found in its different varieties around the world. However, since the first edition, we have increasingly responded to requests from readers to include more information about the majority, nonstandard varieties of English spoken in different parts of the world as well.

Acknowledgements

Very many people have helped with the writing of this book, by supplying information, reading and correcting earlier versions of the typescript, and by advising on content and format. We cannot list them all, but are grateful to all of them. We would particularly like to thank the following: J. Allwood, L. Bauer, A. Bell, J. Bernard, K. Bhat, C. Biggs, J.K. Chambers, J. Clark, A. Davison, J.A. Edmondson, J.R. Edwards, V.K. Edwards, S. Foldvik, E. Gordon, C.W. Kisseberth, Bh. Krishnamurti, L. Lanham, S. Millar, J. Milroy, J.L. Morgan, S.N. Sridhar, D. Sutcliffe, A.R. Thomas, J. Ure, S.K. Verma, J.C. Wells, Jeffrey P. Williams, Jakob Leimgruber and Marie Koh. We are also very grateful to colleagues in the Department of Linguistic Science of Reading University, who helped in many ways.

Symbols

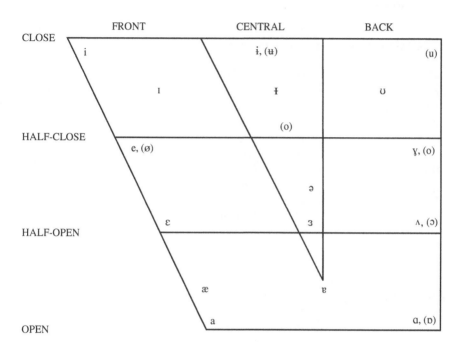

	FRONT	CENTRAL	BACK
CLOSE	i	ɨ, (ʉ)	(u)
	ɪ	ɪ	ʊ
HALF-CLOSE		(o)	
	e, (ø)		ɣ, (o)
		ə	
HALF-OPEN	ɛ	ɜ	ʌ, (ɔ)
	æ	ɐ	
OPEN		a	ɑ, (ɒ)

General symbols

[ ]	—phonetic transcription (indicates actual pronunciation)
/ /	—phonemic transcription
~	—'alternates with'
*	—indicates ungrammatical sentence
?	—indicates sentence of questionable grammaticality

English vowel symbols

A vowel can be described by its position on two dimensions: *open* vs *close*, and *front* vs *back*. This position corresponds roughly to the position in the mouth of the highest point of the tongue in the production of that vowel. Presence of lip rounding is indicated on the diagram opposite by parentheses.

Diacritics

⊤	more open
⊢	more back
⊥	more close
⊣	more front
:	long
·	half-long
´	stress

English consonant phonemes

/p/	as	*p*	in	*peat*
/t/	as	*t*	in	*treat*
/tʃ/	as	*ch*	in	*cheat*
/k/	as	*k*	in	*kite*
/b/	as	*b*	in	*bite*
/d/	as	*d*	in	*date*
/dʒ/	as	*j*	in	*jute*
/g/	as	*g*	in	*gate*
/f/	as	*f*	in	*fate*
/θ/	as	*th*	in	*thought*
/s/	as	*s*	in	*site*
/ʃ/	as	*sh*	in	*sheet*
/h/	as	*h*	in	*hate*
/v/	as	*v*	in	*vote*
/ð/	as	*th*	in	*that*
/z/	as	*z*	in	*zoo*
/ʒ/	as	*s*	in	*vision*
/l/	as	*l*	in	*late*
/r/	as	*r*	in	*rate*
/w/	as	*w*	in	*wait*
/j/	as	*y*	in	*yet*
/m/	as	*m*	in	*meet*
/n/	as	*n*	in	*neat*
/ŋ/	as	*ng*	in	*long*

Other consonant symbols

[ʔ]	glottal stop
[ɫ]	velarized or 'dark' *l*, as in RP *all*
[ɬ]	voiceless lateral fricative
[ɹ]	post-alveolar frictionless continuant, as *r* in RP *right*
[ɾ]	alveolar flap, *r* in Spanish *pero*
[ç]	voiceless palatal fricative

[x]	voiceless velar fricative, as *ch* in German *nacht*
[ɸ]	voiceless bilabial fricative
[ʍ]	voiceless *w*
[ḍ]	voiced alveolar flap
Ç̪	dental consonant
Ç̣	retroflex consonant
Cʰ	aspirated consonant
Ç̩	syllabic consonant

|1|

Standard English in the world

The main subject of this book is *Standard English*. Standard English is the kind of English that this book is written in. There is nothing surprising about this—books, newspapers, magazines and nearly everything else that appears in print in the English-speaking world are written in Standard English. So we have not chosen to write this book in Standard English because we think it is better than other varieties of English, or because it is more expressive or clearer or more logical than other varieties—it isn't. There is quite simply a social convention, which our publisher is keen for us to maintain, that books are not written in any variety of English other than Standard English.

This type of English is called 'standard' because it has undergone standardization, which means that it has been subjected to a process through which it has been selected, codified and stabilized, in a way that other varieties have not.

In the case of certain other languages, 'selected' might mean that an official decision was made at some point for one particular dialect of a language to receive the standardization treatment, as opposed to any of the others. This is not what happened with English. Standard English acquired its status much more gradually and in a more organic way. The ancestor of modern Standard English developed in and around the Royal Court in London, among the aristocracy and ruling elite. Because the elite were concentrated in London, this pre-Standard English was a dialect of a predominantly London-area type. But because it was associated with a group of people who were of mixed geographical origins and who were unusually mobile and well travelled, this court dialect showed signs, from the very earliest records that we have, of being a mixed dialect. For example, the language of the Proclamation of Henry III, a text written as early as 1258, shows a blending of Midland and southern features. And the form of language which eventually emerged over the centuries as the preferred way of writing among the governing classes had features which were not only south-eastern in origin but also southern and Midland, particularly East Midland. And of course the dialect was from the very beginning an upper social class dialect which was not associated with the common workers and peasants.

So no committees were involved in deciding which dialect of English was to be standardized. The upper classes quite naturally wrote in their own dialect, and then were in a position to impose this way of writing on society at large. This was rather widely accepted because the variety was associated with power and status, and had considerable prestige. Even today, although Standard English is the kind of English in which all native speakers learn to read and write, most people do not actually speak it—Standard English is probably not the native dialect of more than about 15 per cent of the population of England. And, reflecting Standard English's social origins, most of that 15 per cent will be concentrated towards the top end of the social scale, so that Standard English is still quite clearly a social dialect—something which is true to a greater or lesser extent of all the English-speaking countries.

As far as codification is concerned, this refers to the fact that Standard English is the variety whose grammar has been described and given public recognition in grammar books and dictionaries, with its norms being widely considered to be 'correct' and constituting 'good usage'. Dictionaries also present norms for spelling. Stabilization means that this type of codification has the effect of ensuring that the variety takes on a relatively uniform and somewhat stable form. However, this uniformity and stability are only relative. The Standard English used in different parts of the native English-speaking world differs noticeably from one place to another, and it is these differences that form the subject matter of this book.

To give some idea of how Standard English differs from other non-standard dialects of the language, we can point out that because of its history and special status, Standard English has a number of grammatical peculiarities which distinguish it from most other varieties. These include:

1. Standard English does not distinguish between the past tense forms of the auxiliary verb *to do* and those of the main verb *to do*. The past tense form in Standard English is *did* in both cases: *You did it, did you?* But in most nonstandard dialects, all over the English-speaking world, *did* is the past tense of the auxiliary, but the main verb has the past tense form *done*: *You done it, did you?*
2. Standard English does not have the grammatical feature which is called negative concord. In most nonstandard varieties, negative forms agree grammatically with one another throughout a clause as in *I couldn't find none nowhere*, where all the words that can take a negative form do so. In Standard English, grammatical agreement or concord of this type does not occur: *I couldn't find any anywhere*.
3. Standard English has an irregular way of forming reflexive pronouns, with some forms based on the possessive pronouns: *myself, yourself, ourselves, yourselves*; and others based on the object pronouns: *himself, themselves*. Many nonstandard dialects have a regular system using

possessive forms throughout i.e. *myself, yourself, hisself, ourselves, your-selves, theirselves*.

4. Standard English has irregular past forms of the verb *to be*, distinguishing between singular and plural, something which does not happen with other verbs: *I was, he was* but *we were, they were*. Most nonstandard dialects have the same form for singular and plural: *I was, she was, we was, you was, they was*; or *I were, he were, we were, you were, they were*.

5. For many irregular verbs, Standard English redundantly distinguishes between past tense and perfect verb forms by using distinct past tense and past participle forms as well as the auxiliary verb *have*: *I have seen him, I could have gone* versus *I saw him, I went*. Many other dialects have no distinction between the past tense and past participle forms, and rely on the presence versus absence of *have* alone: *I have seen him, I could have went* versus *I seen him, I went*.

It is important to stress that the codification and distinctiveness of Standard English do not extend beyond grammar to any other areas of language usage. There is no necessary connection, for instance, between the opposition between standard and nonstandard, and the opposition between formal and informal. Varieties of language viewed from the point of view of relative formality are known technically as *styles*—formal styles are employed in social situations which are formal, and informal styles are employed in informal situations. Stylistic differences in English are mostly conveyed by choice of words, as we can see if we think about the differences between these three sentences:

Father was exceedingly fatigued subsequent to his extensive peregrination
Dad was very tired after his lengthy journey
The old man was bloody knackered after his long trip

Some of the words here, like *was* and *his*, are stylistically neutral; others range from the ridiculously formal *peregrination* through very formal *fatigued* to intermediate *tired* to informal *trip* to very informal (British) *knackered* and tabooed informal *bloody*. But our point here is that the sentence

The old man was bloody knackered after his long trip

is clearly and unambiguously Standard English. Speakers and writers of Standard English have a full range of styles open to them, just as speakers of other varieties do, and can swear and use slang just like anybody else. Equally,

Father were very tired after his lengthy journey

is a sentence in a nonstandard variety of English (from the north of England, perhaps), as we can see from the nonstandard verb form *were*, but it is couched in a rather formal style. Speakers can be informal in Standard English just as they can be formal in nonstandard dialects.

Similarly, there is no connection between Standard English and technical vocabulary. In sociolinguistics, the term *register* refers to a variety of language which is related to topic, subject matter or activity, like the register of mathematics, the register of medicine, or the register of football. And we can certainly acquire and use technical registers without using Standard English, just as we can employ non-technical registers while speaking or writing Standard English. There is no necessary connection between the two. The sentence

There was two eskers what we saw in them U-shaped valleys

is a nonstandard English sentence written in the technical register of physical geography. The sentence

Smith crossed the ball into the box from the byline and Jones just missed with his header

is a Standard English sentence in the register of football (soccer).

Standardization does not extend to pronunciation either. There is no such thing as a Standard English accent. Standard English has nothing to do with accent, and in principle it can be spoken with any pronunciation. In this book, however, we do spend quite a lot of time talking about phonetics and phonology. We discuss only a small proportion of the English accents that are found in the world, concentrating on those accents which most frequently occur together with spoken Standard English. Although there is no connection in principle, as we just said, between the standard variety and any accent, in practice some accents are more likely to be used by the sort of people who are most likely to speak (as opposed to write) Standard English—those of higher social status or educational level. Most of the variation between different varieties of English in the world are to be found at the level of pronunciation, and accents are therefore an important source of both interest and difficulty. For each variety that we discuss, therefore, we treat not only vocabulary and grammar but also pronunciation.

1.1. Models of English

There are three types of country in the world in terms of their relationship to the English language. First, there are nation-states in which English is a *native* language (*ENL*)—where people have English as their mother-tongue, as they do in Australia, Canada, and Ireland. Varieties of English spoken in ENL countries are sometimes also referred to as 'Inner Circle' Englishes. Second, there are countries where English is a *foreign* language (*EFL*), as in Poland, China and Brazil—sometimes known as 'Expanding Circle' nations. These are places where people do not speak English natively and where, if they do speak English, they use it to speak to foreigners. And, third, there are places where English is a *second* language *(ESL)*. In ESL or 'Outer Circle' countries such as India, Pakistan, Nigeria, Kenya, and Singapore, English is not typically spoken as a mother-tongue, but it has some kind of governmental or other official status; it is used as a means of communication within the country, at least among the educated classes; and it is widely employed in the education system, in the newspapers, and in the media generally.

The distinction between ENL, EFL and ESL is by no means absolute. Some varieties of English, for instance, have an interesting recent history of transition from ESL to ENL status. The most obvious example is Southern Irish English. As we point out in Chapter 5, until the nineteenth century, most of the people in much of Ireland were still native-speakers of Irish Gaelic, a Celtic language. The process of language shift whereby most people gradually abandoned Gaelic, so that today Irish people generally are native-speakers of English, has left behind some traces of Gaelic in modern English in central and southern Ireland (SIrEng). Features which would originally have been ESL features, resulting from English having been learnt by people whose native language was Gaelic, are now simply part of native-speaker English in Ireland. For this reason, we can call SIrEng a *shift variety*, meaning that it is the result of relatively recent language shift. There are many other such shift varieties of English where language shift from some other language has had an influence on the linguistic characteristics of the English in question—these include the English spoken in much of Wales, the Shetland Islands, the Scottish Highlands, and the Channel Islands.

ESL Englishes are the subject of Chapter 8, but most of the rest of the book is taken up with accounts of ENL varieties. One of our reasons for doing this is that ENL varieties have typically quite naturally been used as models for people learning EFL, just as people learning, say, German would typically learn it directly or indirectly from native-speakers of German. But because there are so many different varieties of ENL around the world, exposure to one of them does not necessarily equip foreign learners for coping with other varieties when they encounter them. We hope that this book will be of some assistance with this problem.

Of the ENL varieties that are typically used as models in EFL teaching, there are two which have figured most prominently. Traditionally, schools and universities in Europe—and in many other parts of the world—have taught the variety of English which is often referred to as 'British English'. As far as grammar and vocabulary are concerned, this generally means Standard English as it is normally written and spoken by educated speakers in England and, with certain differences, in Wales, Scotland, Northern Ireland, The Republic of Ireland, Australia, New Zealand and South Africa. As far as pronunciation is concerned, it means something much more restrictive, for the RP ('Received Pronunciation') accent which is taught to foreigners is actually used by perhaps only 3–5 per cent of the population of England, and by more or less nobody anywhere else. Like Standard

English, the RP accent has its origins in the south-east of England, but it is currently a social accent associated with the BBC, the public schools in England, and with members of the upper-middle and upper classes. It is true that it also has a history of having considerable prestige in the whole of the British Isles and British Commonwealth, but it is today an accent associated mostly with England. For this reason, in this book we shall refer to the combination of British Standard English grammar and vocabulary with the RP accent as *English* English (EngEng) rather than 'British English'.

The other form of Standard English that is widely taught to students of EFL and ESL is the one we shall refer to as North American English (NAmEng), meaning English as it is written and spoken by educated speakers in the United States of America and Canada. (If we want to distinguish between these two North American varieties, we shall write United States English (USEng) and Canadian English (CanEng).) NAmEng is, naturally, taught to students learning English in North America, and also to those in many parts of Latin America and other areas of the world.

Until recently, many European universities and colleges not only taught EngEng but actually *required* it from their students—other varieties of Standard English were not allowed. This was often the result of a conscious decision that some norm needed to be established and that confusion would arise if teachers offered conflicting models. Lately, very many universities have come to relax this requirement, recognizing that their students are as likely (if not more likely) to encounter NAmEng as EngEng, especially since some European students study for a time in North America. Many universities therefore now permit students to speak and write *either* EngEng *or* NAmEng, *so long as they are consistent* (or that, at least, is the theory).

We feel that this is a step in the right direction but it is also somewhat unrealistic. For example, it is not reasonable to expect a Dutch student of English who has learnt EngEng at school and then studied for a year in the USA to return to the Netherlands with anything other than some mixture of NAmEng and EngEng. This is exactly what happens to British or American native speakers who cross the Atlantic for any length of time. Given that the ideal which foreign students have traditionally aimed at is native-like competence in English, we feel there is nothing at all reprehensible about such a mixture. Nor is it necessarily bad or confusing for schoolchildren to be exposed to more than one model.

In any case, whatever the exact form of the requirements placed on students of English by different universities and in different countries, it is clear that exposure to and/or recognition of the legitimacy of these two varieties of Standard English in English language-learning is likely to bring with it certain problems. Both those teachers wishing to insist on a rigid use of only, say, EngEng to the exclusion of NAmEng and those wishing to permit use of both varieties need to be quite clear about which forms occur in which variety. For example, teachers of EngEng (whether they are native speakers or not) who encounter expressions such as 'First of all . . ., second of all . . .' or 'I did it in five minutes time' in a student's work are likely to regard these as typical learner's mistakes unless they are aware that these forms are perfectly normal in some varieties of NAmEng. Similarly, teachers of NAmEng may mark as incorrect certain forms which are perfectly acceptable in EngEng, such as 'I might do' and 'I'll give it him'.

Of course, NAmEng and EngEng are by no means the only ENL varieties which are used as models in EFL teaching. EFL students in many parts of Asia and Africa are much more likely to come into contact with Australian English (AusEng), New Zealand English (NZEng—jointly AusNZEng), or South African English (SAfEng) than with EngEng or NAmEng. And so it will be useful for students and teachers of English in these areas, too, to be aware of the differences between their standard variety of English and the others.

Another important issue concerns the fact that not only is ENL used as a model in EFL teaching, there has also been a history of employing ENL varieties as teaching models in ESL countries, with some speakers of ESL varieties demonstrating something of an inferiority complex with respect to ENL. There has been a strong feeling in India, for example, that EngEng was the model that should be aimed at in English teaching there, and suggestions to the contrary have been regarded as controversial. Our view is that the days of using EngEng as a model in Asian or African ESL countries should be over. It is very much more sensible to use Standard Indian English as the model in India. Standard Indian English is not only the variety of English used by educated Indians; it is also a well-established and stable variety which is more suitable for use in India than EngEng because speakers of the model variety are close at hand, because its phonology more closely resembles the phonology of Indian languages, and in particular because its vocabulary is adapted to Indian society and culture. The same applies to other ESL countries.

It may well also make sense, on the same kind of grounds, to use ESL models in some EFL contexts. Would it not be a good idea to use West African English as the model in other non-anglophone West African countries such as Senegal and Ivory Coast?

Interestingly, in the past few years this argument about ENL varieties not being the only viable models has now also been extended to discussion as to whether it is always reasonable to use an ENL variety as a model in EFL teaching. It has been pointed out that English now has more non-native than native speakers, and that English is widely used in the modern world as a lingua franca (a language which is used for communication between people who have no native language in common). Very often in the modern world encounters depending on the use of English involve no native speakers at all. Typically, Dutch people travelling to Norway will probably speak English when they get there rather than Dutch or Norwegian; Japanese people are quite likely to speak English to Jordanians; and in multilingual countries like Switzerland, English may even be used at meetings involving only Swiss people. For that reason, it has been suggested that it may not make too much sense always to insist on close adherence to native-speaker models, especially where these cause difficulty. Why should Italians spend hours of effort mastering the English *th* sounds if they are going to be speaking English to Russians who cannot pronounce these sounds either? Does it matter if Polish people say *The possibility to solve this problem* (rather than *The possibility of solving this problem* as ENL speakers would), if they are talking to Finns who would probably make the same mistake themselves?

In fact, it may be that there are developing in some parts of the world varieties that we can call *ELF*—English as a lingua franca—in the sense that, say, the way Europeans speak English to each other may be taking on a relatively stable common form, different from EngEng, which could be described and taught to learners if they so wish. If there is, or were to be, a European ELF, we can expect that it would probably lack features which ELF learners typically find difficult to acquire, and have features corresponding to points where English differs from most other European languages. It might, for example, lack third-person singular -*s*, and use the word *actually* to mean 'at the moment'. If so, then such ELF varieties could be analysed and described by linguists, and used as teaching models if teachers and learners wanted this.

We will not be dealing further in this book with possible ELF varieties. One of the main aims of this book is to describe ENL (and ESL) varieties in order to facilitate the comprehension of these different varieties by EFL speakers, whichever variety they happen to have learnt themselves. Since it is difficult to imagine that there might be many EFL speakers in the world, if any at all, who will never encounter and want to understand ENL (and ESL) Englishes, at least in the electronic media, this would not be relevant. But even if no one ultimately decides to use an ELF variety as a model, this discussion does remind us that, in teaching EFL, some features of English are more important than others, and priorities have to be considered—the English *th* sounds are not really very important in terms of the role they play in the language, and even a number of ENL varieties do not have them.

1.2. The spread of English

The English language developed out of Germanic dialects that were brought to Britain, during the course of the fifth and sixth centuries, by the Jutes (from modern Jutland, Denmark), Angles (from modern Schleswig, Denmark/Germany), Saxons (from modern Holstein, Germany), and Frisians (from modern Friesland, Netherlands/Germany). By mediaeval times, this Germanic language had replaced the original Celtic language of Britain in nearly all of England, as well as in southern and eastern Scotland. Until the 1600s, however, English remained a language spoken by a relatively small number of people in the world, and was confined geographically to the island of Britain. Indeed, even much of Britain remained non-English-speaking. The original Celtic language of Britain survived in the form of Welsh in nearly all of Wales and as Cornish in much of Cornwall. The Highlands and Islands of western and northern Scotland spoke Gaelic, another Celtic language which had been brought across from Ireland in pre-mediaeval times. And the populations of the Northern Isles—Orkney and Shetland—still spoke the Scandinavian language, Norn, which they had inherited from their Viking ancestors. It was not until the seventeenth century that the English language began the geographical and demographic expansion which has led to the situation in which it finds itself today, with more non-native speakers than any other language in the world, and more native speakers than any other language except Chinese.

This expansion began in the late 1600s, with the arrival of English-speakers in the Americas—North America (the modern United States and Canada), Bermuda, the Bahamas, and the Caribbean—and the importation of English, from Scotland, into the northern areas of Ireland. Subsequently, during the 1700s, English also began to penetrate into southern Ireland, and it was during this time, too, that Cornish finally disappeared from Cornwall, and Norn from Orkney and Shetland. During the 1800s, English began making serious inroads into Wales, so that today only 20 per cent of the population of that country are native Welsh-speakers; and in the Highlands and islands of Scotland, English also began to replace Gaelic, which today has around 60,000 native-speakers, down from 80,000 in 1970.

It was also during the 1800s that the development of Southern Hemisphere varieties of English began. During the early nineteenth century, large-scale colonization of Australia began to take place and, at a slightly later date, New Zealand, South Africa and the Falkland Islands also began to be colonized from the British Isles. The South Atlantic islands of St Helena and Tristan da Cunha also acquired English-speaking populations during the 1800s, as did Pitcairn Island and, subsequently, Norfolk Island in the South Pacific (see Chapter 7).

Not surprisingly, these patterns of expansion, settlement and colonization have had an effect on the relationships, similarities and differences between the varieties of English which have grown up in different parts of the world. For example, there are very many similarities between Scottish (ScotEng) and northern Irish English (NIrEng). NAmEng and the English of southern Ireland (SIrEng) also have many points of similarity. And the English varieties of the Southern Hemisphere (Australia, New Zealand, South Africa, Falklands), which were transplanted relatively recently from the British Isles, are very similar to each other. They are quite naturally much less different from the English of England than are the varieties spoken in the Americas, which were settled much earlier. Welsh English (WEng), too, is structurally very similar to EngEng, although as a shift variety the influence of Welsh has played a role in its formation.

These differences and similarities are most obvious at the level of pronunciation. Varieties of English around the world differ relatively little in their consonant systems, and most differences can be observed at the level of vowel systems. Even here, differences are not enormous. The most distinctive varieties in terms of their vowel systems are: (a) those of Scotland

and northern Ireland (see Chapter 5); and (b) those of the Caribbean. The distinctiveness of Scottish and northern Irish English reflect ancient differences between northern and southern British varieties of English, which in some cases go back to pre-mediaeval times. The distinctiveness of the Caribbean varieties, on the other hand, reflects the influence of African languages and of the process of creolization (see Chapter 6) in their formation.

We have attempted to portray the relationships between the pronunciations of the major non-Caribbean varieties in Figure 1.1. This diagram is somewhat arbitrary and slightly misleading (there are, for example, accents of USEng which are closer to RP than to mid-western US English), but it does show the two main types of pronunciation: an 'English' type (EngEng, WEng, SAfEng, AusEng, NZEng) and an 'American' type (USEng, CanEng), with IrEng falling somewhere between the two and ScotEng being somewhat by itself.

Lexically and grammatically, the split between the 'English' and 'American' types is somewhat neater, with USEng and CanEng being opposed on most counts to the rest of the English-speaking world. This generalization holds true in spite of the fact that each variety has its individual lexical and grammatical characteristics and that, for instance, at some points where ScotEng and IrEng grammar differ from EngEng, they closely resemble NAmEng.

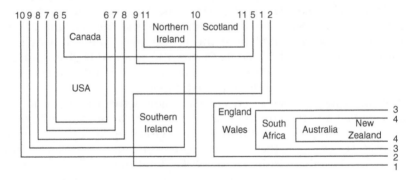

Fig. 1.1.
Key
1. /ɑ:/ rather than /æ/ in *path* etc.
2. absence of non-prevocalic /r/
3. close vowels for /æ/ and /ɛ/, monophthongization of /ai/ and /au/
4. front [a:] for /ɑ:/ in *part* etc.
5. absence of contrast of /ɒ/ and /ɔ:/ as in *cot* and *caught*
6. /æ/ rather than /ɑ:/ in *can't* etc.
7. absence of contrast of /ɒ/ and /ɑ:/ as in *bother* and *father*
8. consistent voicing of intervocalic /t/
9. unrounded [ɑ] in *pot*
10. syllabic /r/ in *bird*
11. absence of contrast of /ʊ/ and /u:/ as in *pull* and *pool*

The 'English' types of English, which do not differ greatly from EngEng, will be treated first in this book and are discussed in Chapter 2. The 'American' types, and the relatively larger amount of differences between them and the 'English' types, are dealt with, necessarily at greater length, in Chapters 3 and 4. ScotEng and IrEng, which we classify as neither 'English' nor 'American' types, are discussed in Chapter 5.

Of native varieties of English spoken in other areas (see Chapter 7), Bermudian English is more of the 'American' type, while the Englishes spoken on Tristan da Cunha and the Falkland Islands are more of the 'English' type, the latter bearing some resemblances to AusEng.

English-based pidgins and creoles, which are discussed in Chapter 6, have a much more complex history than other English varieties. They include the Atlantic pidgins, creoles and pidginized varieties of the Caribbean area, the Atlantic coasts of North, Central and South America, the island of St Helena, and West Africa; and the Pacific varieties of Papua New Guinea, the Solomon Islands, and Vanuatu, among others. American Black Vernacular English also has a creole history, and there are transplanted off-shoots of it in Liberia and the Dominican Republic. As we have noted, there are also well-established second-language varieties of English such as those found in Africa, Malaysia and the Indian subcontinent. Chapter 7 discusses these ESL varieties.

1.3. The nature of native overseas Englishes

One very interesting question for linguists is why the native forms of English which have developed outside Britain are like they are. If you take English from Britain and introduce it elsewhere, why does it end up being recognizably different from English in the original homeland? One obvious factor has to do with linguistic change. All languages and dialects change through time: some changes have taken place since settlement in the English of particular overseas territories; and, equally, some changes have taken place in Britain which have not taken place in all or any of the new territories. Of the features outlined in Figure 1.1., numbers 1, 2, 5, 8 and 11 are innovations which have taken place in some areas but not others. For example, feature 2, the absence of non-prevocalic /r/—the pronunciation of words such as *cart* without an /r/—represents an innovation, in which the /r/ was lost, which occurred in southern England; the innovation then spread to certain other areas but not all of them.

Another factor is language contact—in the new territories, speakers of English came into contact with indigenous languages from which they acquired words, as well as with other European languages. In New Zealand, for example, English speakers encountered the Polynesian language Maori (see 2.2.2.5.), which has subsequently had a considerable influence on NZEng. Irish Gaelic had an effect on IrEng (see 5.2.7.). In the USA, English-speakers met speakers of indigenous Amerindian languages, as well as Spanish and French and, as a result of the slave trade, African

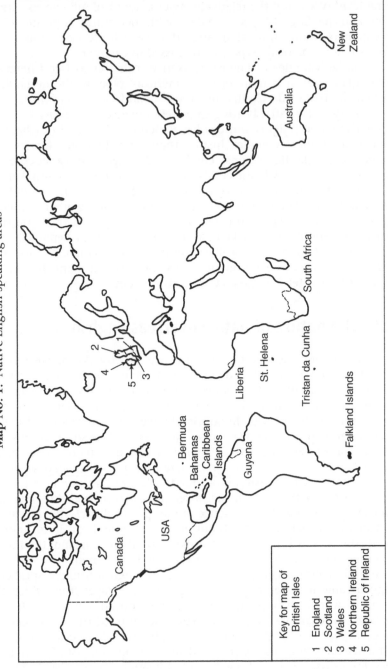

Map No. 1. Native English-speaking areas

Canada

USA

Bermuda
Bahamas
Caribbean
Islands

Guyana

Liberia

St. Helena

Tristan da Cunha

South Africa

Falkland Islands

Australia

New
Zealand

1
2
3
4
5

Key for map of
British Isles

1 England
2 Scotland
3 Wales
4 Northern Ireland
5 Republic of Ireland

languages (see 4.3.); later on, many speakers of German, Yiddish and other European languages arrived, something which had a clear effect on the vocabulary and maybe even on the syntax of USEng—some of the grammatical differences between EngEng and USEng, such as the one discussed in 4.1.1.4.(2) *I like skating* versus *I like to skate*, may be accounted for by German influence.

Finally, dialect contact was very important. In the new colonies, speakers of different regional varieties of English from different parts of England, Scotland, Wales and Ireland came into contact with one another and, in a generation or two, this gave rise to new varieties which were essentially mixtures of features from different homeland dialects. Feature 5, for example, the merger of the vowels of *cot* and *caught*, probably arrived in Canada from Scotland, while, on the other hand, Canada does not have the Scottish merger of *pull* and *pool*, preserving here the contrast typical of EngEng. Dialect mixture also led to a levelling out of many dialect differences: there is much less regional variation in the overseas varieties than there is in England and Scotland. In Britain you can often tell where someone comes from by the way they speak to within, say, 15 km. In eastern North America it is often more like 200 km; and in western North America, and in Australia, it is hardly possible at all.

|2|

English, Australasian, South African and Welsh English

In this chapter we discuss the 'English' types of English and point out the relationships and differences between them. At certain points we also contrast and compare the 'English' types with NAmEng, but this is done in more detail in Chapters 3 and 4.

2.1. The RP accent

As we have already mentioned, the accent which is normally taught to students who are studying EngEng is the accent known as RP. This is also the accent which is described in Cruttenden and Gimson (2008) and in most other British textbooks. There are a number of advantages to learning this particular accent. First, while it originated in the south-east of England, it is now a genuinely regionless accent within England, i.e. if speakers have an RP accent, you cannot tell which area of England they come from, which is not the case for any other type of British accent. This means that this accent is likely to be encountered throughout the country. Second, RP and accents similar to it are quite often used in radio and television broadcasts in England, so a student will have many opportunities to listen to them.

There are also disadvantages to learning only RP. First, it is an accent used natively by only 3–5 per cent of the population of England. This means that students arriving in England for the first time may have difficulty—sometimes a great deal of difficulty—in understanding the other 95–97 per cent of the population. (One book which attempts to help with this problem is Hughes, Trudgill and Watt, 2005.) Second, while RP is not a regional accent, it *is* a social accent, associated particularly with the upper-middle and upper classes (and those who aspire to membership of those classes). Foreigners who are very successful at acquiring an RP accent may therefore be treated as if they were upper-class—and the reaction might not *always* be favourable! Third, the RP accent is probably rather more difficult for many foreigners to acquire than, say, a Scottish accent, since RP has a large number of diphthongs and a not particularly close relationship to English orthography.

2.1.1. The RP vowel system

The RP vowel system is presented in Table 2.1 and can also be heard on the recording. While RP does not have any regional variation, as we have said, it does have variation of other types. In particular, there is variation between what some writers have called 'conservative' and 'advanced' RP (see Cruttenden and Gimson, 2008, and Wells, 1982). For the most part this reflects linguistic changes that are currently taking place in RP, with 'conservative' pronunciations being most typical of older speakers and 'advanced' pronunciations typical of younger speakers. Some of these differences are the following:

1. As in a number of other accents, the distinction between /ɔə/ and /ɔ:/ is now lost for very many speakers, with /ɔə/ becoming monophthongized. A more recent, but by now also widespread development, is the loss of /ʊə/ and the merger of this diphthong, also, with /ɔ:/. This latter change for some speakers has affected some words but not others,

Table 2.1. The RP vowel system*

/ɪ/	*bid, very, mirror, wanted, horses, honest*
/ɛ/	*bed, merry*
/æ/	*bad, marry*
/ɒ/	*pot, long, cough, horrid*
/ʌ/	*putt, hurry*
/ʊ/	*put*
/i:/	*bee*
/ei/	*bay*
/ai/	*buy*
/ɔi/	*boy*
/u:/	*boot*
/ou/	*boat*
/ɑu/	*bout*
/ɪə/	*peer, idea*
/ɛə/	*pair, Mary*
/ʊə/	*poor*
/ɔə/	*pore*
/ɔ:/	*paw, port, talk, boring*
/ɑ:/	*bard, path, dance, half, banana, father, calm*
/ɜ:/	*bird, furry*
/ə/	*about, sofa, butter*
/aiə/	*fire*
/ɑuə/	*tower*

*The words in Table 2.1. are also used in the recording for WIEng, WAfEng and IndEng.

so that *sure* may be /ʃɔ:/ but *poor*, /pʊə/. The current situation with respect to these vowels is something like this:

	paw	*pore*	*poor*
older speakers	/ɔ:/	/ɔə/	/ʊə/
middle-aged speakers	/ɔ:/	/ɔ:/	/ʊə/
younger speakers	/ɔ:/	/ɔ:/	/ɔ:/

2. There is a strong tendency, perhaps part of the same process whereby /ɔə/>/ɔ:/, for original triphthongs formed from /ai/ and /au/ plus /ə/ to be pronounced as monophthongs, e.g. *tower* /tauə/>/tɑ:/. This process can be labelled *smoothing* (see Wells, 1982).
3. Where orthographic *o* occurs before the voiceless fricatives /f/, /θ/z/s/, older speakers sometimes pronounce the vowel as /ɔ:/, e.g. *off* /ɔ:f/, *froth* /frɔ:θ/, *lost* /lɔ:st/. This pronunciation is currently dying out in RP and being replaced by /ɒ/. Words like *salt* and *fault* may also pronounced with /ɔ:/, but are often pronounced with /ɒ/, too, by younger speakers.
4. Conservative RP has a back vowel [u:] in words like *boot*, but for younger speakers the vowel may increasingly be fronted in the direction of [ʉ:] except before /l/, as in *fool*.
5. The diphthong /ou/ of *boat* varies considerably, ranging from [ɔʊ] among conservative speakers to [øʉ] among some advanced speakers. Perhaps the most neutral pronunciation is around [əu].
6. The diphthong /ɛə/ of *pair* is very often monophthongized to [ɛ:] (cf. 1. and 2. above).
7. Words like *suit* may be pronounced either /su:t/ or /sju:t/. The tendency is for middle-aged and younger speakers to omit the /j/ after /s/ before /u:/, but this tendency is much stronger in some words, e.g. *super*, *Susan*, than in others, e.g. *suit*. Word-internally, /j/ tends to be retained, as in *assume* /əsju:m/. There is also fluctuation after /l/: word-initially *lute* /lu:t/ is normal, but it is possible to pronounce, for example, *illusion* as /ɪlju:ʒn/.
8. There is an increasing tendency for /ʊ/, as in *put*, to be pronounced with an unrounded vowel [ɣ].

2.1.2. Vowels in near-RP accents

Since RP speakers make up a very small percentage of the English population, many native speakers working as teachers of English are not native speakers of RP. If they are from the south of England, particularly the south-east, it is likely that their accents will closely *resemble* RP (especially if they are of middle-class origin), but not be identical to it. Typical differences between the RP vowel system and many near-RP south-of-England accents are the following:

1. The /i:/ of *bee*, rather than the /ɪ/ of *bid*, occurs in the final syllable of *very*, *many*, etc. in the near-RP accents. In this respect, these accents

resemble NAmEng, SAfEng and AusNZEng. This feature is currently spreading geographically in England, from north to south, and it is also showing signs that it will become established as the most usual RP pronunciation in the near future.

2. The fronting of /u:/ towards [ʉ:] is more widespread than in RP. Thus the allophone of /u:/ before /l/, which is not fronted in either type of accent, is, in near-RP, markedly different from those allophones that occur in all other environments. Unlike advanced RP, this variation of allophones with respect of /l/ also occurs with the diphthong /ou/. Thus:

	rude	*rule*	*code*	*coal*
Conservative RP	[ru:d]	[ru:ɫ]	[kɔud]	[kɔuɫ]
Advanced RP	[rʉ:d]	[ru:ɫ]	[køʉd]	[køʉɫ]
Near-RP, southern	[rʉ:d]	[ru:ɫ]	[køud]	[kɔuɫ]

3. The vowel /ɪ/ in unstressed syllables in RP often corresponds to /ə/ in near-RP accents. The actual distribution of /ɪ/ and /ə/ varies considerably among the different near-RP accents. By way of illustration, there are some near-RP accents which have /ɪ/ in *hon<u>e</u>st*, *vill<u>a</u>ge*, but /ə/ in *want<u>e</u>d*, *hors<u>e</u>s*. In these accents, therefore, the RP distinction between *roses* /rouzɪz/ and *Rosa's* /rouzəz/ (also found in many NAmEng accents) does not occur, both forms being /rouzəz/.

4. Speakers with northern near-RP accents are likely to differ from RP in one important phonological respect. Like RP, they have a contrast between /æ/ and /ɑ:/ as demonstrated by the following pairs:

/æ/	/ɑ:/
pat	*part*
Pam	*palm*
match	*march*

However, there are two groups of words where RP has /ɑ:/ but northern accents have /æ/. These are:

(a) words in which RP has /ɑ:/ where orthographic *a* is followed by the voiceless fricatives /f/, /θ/, or /s/: *laugh, path, grass*;

(b) words in which RP has /ɑ:/ where orthographic *a* is followed by the nasal clusters /nt/, /ns/, /nʃ/, /nd/ and /mp/: *plant, dance, branch, demand, sample*. (Note that southern EngEng has *branch* as /brɑ:nʃ/, northern EngEng /bræntʃ/.)

5. Some speakers from the Midlands and north of England may have local accents which lack the vowel /ʌ/ of *putt* and *hurry*. In such accents words such as these have the vowel /ʊ/ instead, with the consequence that *but* and *put* are perfect rhymes: /bʊt/, /pʊt/.

2.1.3. RP consonants

1. /l/. One feature of the RP accent, which it shares with many other EngEng accents and those of other 'English' varieties but is not found

in NAmEng, ScotEng or IrEng, concerns the positional allophones of the consonant *l*. Syllable-initial /l/ as in *lot* is 'clear', i.e. pronounced with the body of the tongue raised towards the hard palate, giving a front vowel resonance, while syllable-final /l/ as in *hill* and syllabic /l/ as in *bottle* are 'dark' or velarized, i.e. pronounced with the body of the tongue raised towards the soft palate, giving a back-vowel resonance. Thus *lull* /lʌl/ is pronounced [lʌɫ]. (This difference also holds in AusNZEng. For NAmEng, IrEng and ScotEng, see Chapters 3 and 5.) Note that in certain non-RP south-of-England accents, [ɫ] may be considerably darker than in RP or even become vocalized, e.g. *hill* [hɪʊ].

2. /ʍ/. Most EngEng accents have lost the original /w/:/ʍ/ contrast as in *witch : which*, *Wales : whales*. This is for the most part true also of RP, but there are some (especially older) RP speakers who still preserve it, and one suspects this is often the result of a conscious decision and effort to do so.

3. [ʔ]. In many varieties of English in the British Isles (i.e. EngEng, NIrEng, ScotEng), the consonant /t/ may be realized as a glottal stop [ʔ], except at the beginning of a stressed syllable. This usage of the glottal stop is known technically as 'glottaling'. Thus:

top   [top]
between   [bɪtwi:n]
bitter   [bɪtə~bɪʔə]
fit   [fɪt~fɪʔ]

In RP itself, the glottal stop can appear only in the following two environments:

(a) as a realization of syllable-final /t/ before a following consonant, as in:

fit them   [fɪtðəm~fɪʔðəm]
batman   [bætmn̩~bæʔmn̩]

This is a relatively recent development in RP and is most often heard from younger speakers. It is variable in its occurrence and occurs more frequently before some consonants (e.g. /m/) than others (e.g. /h/). In RP /t/ is *not* realized as [ʔ] between two vowels in environments such as *bitter* or *fit us*.

(b) [ʔ] occurs before /tʃ/ and in certain consonant clusters, as in *church* [tʃɜ:ʔtʃ], *box* [bɒʔks], *simply* [sɪmʔplɪ], where it is known as 'glottal reinforcement' or 'glottalization'.

Neither of these types of pronunciation is normally taught to foreigners, but students should be aware of them. It is probable that the occurrence of [ʔ] in words like those in (b), in particular, helps lead to the impression many North Americans have that the RP accents sounds 'clipped'; and that its absence in either environment contributes to the 'foreignness' of non-native accents.

4. /r/.

(a) As is well-known, some English accents are 'rhotic' or 'r-ful' and others are 'non-rhotic' or 'r-less'. Rhotic accents are those which actually pronounce /r/, corresponding to orthographic *r*, in words like *far* and *farm*: /fɑːr/, /fɑːrm/. The consonant *r* in these positions—word-finally before a pause, or before a consonant—is known as 'non-prevocalic /r/'. Most of south-western England, together with part of Lancashire in the north-west, have rhotic accents. Non-rhotic accents do not have /r/ in these positions and have, for example, *farm* as /fɑːm/. Most of southern and eastern EngEng regional accents are non-rhotic. RP is a non-rhotic accent, and thus has no contrasts of the type:

ma   *mar*
cawed   *cord*

(b) Speakers of many non-rhotic accents, while not pronouncing ortho-graphic *r* word-finally before a pause or before a consonant, do pro-nounce it where there is a following word which begins with a vowel:

It's not far	no /r/
He's far behind	no /r/
She's far away	/r/ pronounced

That is to say, words like *far* have two pronunciations, depending on whether or not there is a following vowel. In non-rhotic accents, the /r/ that occurs in *far away*, etc. is known as *linking /r/*. The RP accent has this linking /r/. Failure by students to pronounce linking /r/ does not usually affect comprehension but may result in their sounding stilted or foreign. Note, however, that not all non-rhotic accents of English have linking /r/—see Table 2.2.

(c) As a further development, and by analogy with linking /r/, there are now many accents of English in which an /r/ is inserted before a fol-lowing vowel even though there is no *r* in the spelling. This /r/ is

Table 2.2. /r/

	for Non-prevocalic /r/	*for it* Linking /r/	*saw it* Intrusive /r/
RP	no	yes	variable
Non-RP, South EngEng	no	yes	yes
ScotEng	yes	—	no
IrEng	yes	—	no
CanEng	yes	—	no
Mid-West USEng	yes	—	no
Northeastern USEng	no	yes	yes
Lower Southern USEng	no	no	no
AusEng	no	yes	yes
NZEng	no	yes	yes
SAfEng	no	no	no

known as *intrusive* /r/. In many EngEng accents it occurs in environments such as:

draw	/drɔ:/	*draw up*	/drɔ:rʌp/
	on the pattern of *soar—soar up*		
pa	/pɑ:/	*pa and*	/pɑ:rənd/
	on the pattern of *far—far and*		
China	/tʃainə/	*China and*	/tʃainərənd/
	on the pattern of *finer—finer and*		
idea	/aidɪə/	*idea and*	/aidɪərənd/
	on the pattern of *near—near and*		

It can also occur word-internally, as in *drawing* /drɔ:rɪŋ/. Obviously, what has happened historically is that the loss of /r/ before consonants in non-rhotic accents, which led to alternations of the *far—far away* type, has become reinterpreted as a rule which inserts /r/ after the vowels /ɑ:/, /ɔ:/, /ɜ:/, /ɪə/, /ɛə/ and /ə/, before a following vowel.

Does RP have intrusive /r/? Many textbooks suggest that it does not. The actual situation, however, is that today most RP speakers, particularly younger ones, do have intrusive /r/ after /ə/, as in *China and*, and after /ɪə/, as in *idea of*. In these environments, pronunciations without /r/ sound stilted or foreign. In other environments, as in *law and*, *pa and*, *drawing*, while intrusive /r/ does occur in the non-RP accents, particularly those spoken in the south-east of England, it is still somewhat conspicuous in RP. Intrusive /r/ in these environments is still socially stigmatized to a certain extent—the /r/ is felt to be 'incorrect' because it does not correspond to an *r* in the spelling—and many RP speakers try to avoid it, quite frequently without being entirely successful. For example, many BBC newsreaders, when reading a phrase such as *law and order*, have to pause or insert a glottal stop before *and* in order not to pronounce an /r/.

Table 2.2 gives some indication of the occurrence of these different /r/s in different varieties of English.

2.2. Australian, New Zealand and South African English

We now turn to an examination of the other 'English' types of English, and first the Southern Hemisphere varieties of Australia, New Zealand and South Africa. Strange as it may seem to those who speak these varieties, many people from other parts of the English-speaking world often have difficulty in telling one from the other—and indeed, as we have already suggested, there are many similarities between them in spite of the thousands of miles that separate the three countries.

The sociolinguistic situation (as far as English is concerned) is also similar in the three countries. There is, for example, very little regional variation in the English used, especially if compared to the amount of regional variation found in Britain—although there is probably rather more variation of this type in SAfEng than in the other two countries. (For the most part, regional variation in AusNZEng is lexical.) There is, on the other hand, a fair amount of social variation in all three types. This variation may be described as involving—as far as pronunciation is concerned—'mild' and 'broad' accents. While all AusNZEng and SAfEng accents are phonologically very close to RP, phonetically there are considerable differences: the 'mild' accents differ somewhat from RP, while the 'broad' accents differ considerably from RP. The 'mild' accents tend to be found towards the top of the social scale, particularly amongst older speakers. (RP is an accent which still has some prestige in these three countries, but there has been a very marked decline in this prestige in the past fifty years or so.)

2.2.1. AusEng

English has been spoken in Australia since 1788, where it currently has about 20 million native speakers.

2.2.1.1. AusEng vowels: phonological differences from RP vowels

1. Like south-of-England non-RP accents, AusEng has /iː/ rather than /ɪ/ in *very*, *many*, etc. Thus, *seedy* has the same vowel in both syllables in AusEng, while the vowels in *city* differ (see 2.1.2.(1)).
2. Like south-of-England non-RP accents, but to a much greater extent, AusEng has /ə/ rather than /ɪ/ in unstressed syllables. Thus, not only does /ə/ occur in the final syllable of *horses* and *wanted*, it also occurs in the final syllable of *naked, David, honest, village*, etc. (see 2.1.2.(3)). This applies also in the unstressed syllables in words such as *begin* /bəgɪn/ and *laxity* /læksətiː/. This feature is known, following Wells (1982), as the Weak Vowel Merger—a diagnostic of this is that words such as *rabbit* and *abbot* rhyme.
3. AusEng follows RP in having /ɑː/ in *laugh, path, grass*, etc., but it differs from RP, and is more like non-RP north-of-England accents, in often having /æ/ in *dance, sample, plant, branch*, etc. (see 2.1.2.(4)). There is, however, a certain amount of regional variation. The individual word *castle* often has /æ/ in New South Wales and Queensland, while words from the *dance* set often have /ɑː/ in South Australia. There is also some social variation. Other things being equal, /ɑː/ forms are considered somewhat more prestigious then /æ/ forms.
4. RP smoothing of /aʊə/>/ɑː/, etc., does not occur (see 2.1.1.(2)).

2.2.1.2. AusEng vowels: phonetic differences from RP vowels

Phonetic differences between RP and AusEng are considerable and, of course, most noticeable in 'broad' Australian accents. In some respects AusEng pronunciation resembles that of the London area of England more than RP, but there are many dissimilarities also. These phonetic differences are most obvious in the case of vowels, which are shown in Table 2.3.

Table 2.3. Phonetic differences between broad AusEng and RP vowels

		RP	Broad AusEng
bid	/ɪ/	[ɪ]	[i̝]
bed	/ɛ/	[ɛ]	[e̝]
bad	/æ/	[æ]	[ɛ̝]
pot	/ɒ/	[ɒ]	[ɔ̝]
putt	/ʌ/	[ɐ]	[ɐ˧]
put	/ʊ/	[ʊ]	[ʊ]
bee	/iː/	[i̝i]	[ɜ·ɪ]
bay	/ei/	[eɪ]	[a̝·ɪ]
buy	/ai/	[aɪ]	[ɒ·ɪ]~[ɒ·ə]
boy	/ɔi/	[ɔɪ]	[o·ɪ]
boot	/uː/	[u̝u]	[ʉʉ˧]
boat	/ou/	[ɵu]	[ɒ·ʉ~[ɐ·ə]
bout	/ɑu/	[ɑʊ]	[æ·ʉ]~[æ·^{ɒ}]~[ɛ·u̝]
peer	/ɪə/	[ɪə]	[i̝ː]
pair	/ɛə/	[ɛə]	[e̝ː]
paw	/ɔː/	[ɔː]	[*o*ː]~[oɐ]
bard	/ɑː/	[ɑː]	[aː]
bird	/ɜː/	[ɜː]	[əː]

Although we are concentrating in this book on varieties employed by more educated speakers, it is possible in the case of AusNZEng and SAfEng accents to give more information by illustrating those varieties most unlike RP—i.e. 'broad' accents. 'Milder' accents are then those that are intermediate between 'broad' accents and RP.

The distinctive differences are:

1. AusEng front vowels tend to be closer than in RP (i.e. the body of the tongue is closer to the palate). For example, *bid* can sound more like [bid].
2. Some of the diphthongs are wider than in RP (i.e. the difference between the open first element and closed second element is greater in AusEng than in RP), but there is much social variation in the quality of the first element.
3. There is a tendency for the diphthong to be 'slower', i.e. with a longer first element, than in RP, and even for diphthongs to become monophthongized, as in /ai/ as [ɒ·ɪ~ɒ·^{ɪ}~ɒ·^{ə}].
4. The /ɑː/ vowel is a very front [aː] in comparison to most other varieties of English.
5. Word-final /ə/ is often very open, e.g. *ever* [evɐ].
6. The /ʊ/ vowel usually receives much more lip-rounding than in EngEng.

2.2.1.3. AusEng consonants
For AusEng consonants, we can note the following:

1. AusEng is non-rhotic and has linking and intrusive /r/ (see 2.1.3.(4)). AusEng /r/ is often more strongly retroflexed than in EngEng.
2. Intervocalic /t/ as in *city*, *better*, may become the voiced flap—[d̪], as in NAmEng. However, this is by no means so common, standard, or consistent as it is in NAmEng, and [t] is also frequent in this environment. The glottal stop realization of /t/ may occur in *fit them*, as in RP, but not in any other environment. Glottal reinforcement as in *box*, *batch* does not occur (see 2.1.3.(3)).
3. AusEng often has an /l/ that is darker than in RP, e.g. *leaf* [ɫɜɪf].

2.2.1.4. Other AusEng pronunciation features
1. *Assume* etc. may be pronounced as /əʃúːm/ rather than /əsúːm/~/əsjúːm/. Similarly, *presume* etc. can have /ʒ/ rather than /z/ or /zj/.
2. In some areas, /ɔː/ may be heard in *off*, *often*, etc. more frequently than in RP.
3. *Australia*, *auction*, *salt*, which may have /ɒ/ or /ɔː/ in RP, have only /ɒ/ in AusEng (see 2.1.1.(3)).
4. Days of the week tend to be pronounced with final /eɪ/ rather than RP /ɪ/, especially by younger speakers: *Monday* /mʌndeɪ/.
5. Initial /tj/, /dj/ may be pronounced as [tʃ], [dʒ], e.g. *tune* [tʃə·ʉn], though this is not especially common in educated usage. (This feature is also found in many BritEng varieties.)
6. The sequence /lj/ often becomes /j/, as in *brilliant* (cf. 3.2.5.).
7. *Memo* is pronounced /miːmou/, not /mɛmou/, as elsewhere.

2.2.1.5. Grammatical differences between AusEng and EngEng
At the level of educated speech and writing, there are very few obvious grammatical differences between AusEng and EngEng. It is not usually possible to tell if a text has been written by an English or Australian writer—unless by the vocabulary (see below). There are, however, a few distinctive tendencies:

1. The use of the auxiliaries *shall* and *should* with first-person subjects, as in *I shall go, We should like to see you*, is less usual in AusEng than in EngEng, and even in EngEng these are now increasingly replaced by *will* and *would*, as in *I will go/I'll go, We would like to see you*.
2. In EngEng, the following negative forms of *used to* are all possible:

    He used not to go
    He usedn't to go
    He didn't use to go

    with the first (older and more formal) construction being the most usual in writing. In AusEng, the third form is less usual than in

EngEng, while the second form is probably more usual than in EngEng. Contracted forms without *to*—*He usedn't go*—are also more usual in AusEng than in EngEng.

3. For some speakers of EngEng, the auxiliary *do* is normally used in tag questions in sentences with the auxiliary *ought*: *He ought to go, didn't he?* In AusEng, *do* is not used in such cases; instead, *should* or *ought* would occur (i.e. *shouldn't he?, oughtn't he?* in the above sentence).

4. The use of *have* in expressing possession, as in *I have a new car*, is more usual in EngEng than in AusEng, where *got*, as in *I've got a new car*, is preferred.

5. EngEng permits all the following double-object constructions (with some regional variation):

I'll give it him
I'll give him it
I'll give it to him

The construction with *to* is probably the most frequent in EngEng, especially in the south of England, and it is this form which is the most usual in AusEng (see also 4.1.1.4.).

6. In EngEng, it is quite usual for collective nouns to take plural verbs:

The government have made a mistake
The team are playing very badly

The reverse is the usual case in AusEng, where the above two sentences would tend to have the singular forms *has* and *is*, respectively (see also 4.1.2.2.).

7. In colloquial AusEng, the feminine pronoun *she* can be used to refer to inanimate nouns and in impersonal constructions:

She'll be right ('Everything will be all right')
She's a stinker today ('The weather is excessively hot today')

8. In some constructions AusEng may use an infinitive rather than a participle: *Some people delay to pay their tax* (cf. 4.1.1.4.).

9. USEng-style adverbial placement may occur: *He already has done it* (see 4.1.3.).

10. AusEng, like USEng, may have, for example, *Have you ever gone to London?* where EngEng would often prefer *Have you ever been to London?*

11. Some AusEng speakers use *whenever* to refer to a single occasion, as in NIrEng (see 5.2.2.).

12. The past participle forms *known, blown, sown, mown, grown, thrown, shown, flown*, are often pronounced with final /ən/ rather than /n/, e.g. *known* /nouən/.

2.2.1.6. Lexical differences between EngEng and AusEng

Vocabulary differences between the Australasian varieties and EngEng are relatively small when compared to differences between the 'English' and

'American' varieties. They are, however, numerous enough at the level of colloquial vocabulary. Some of the differences between EngEng and AusEng vocabulary are the result of borrowings into AusEng from Australian aboriginal languages. Well-known examples of such loans include *boomerang, dingo* (a wild dog) and *billabong* (a cut-off river channel), as well as many names for indigenous flora and fauna. In other cases the differences are purely intra-English. We give a short list of these below by way of illustration of types of lexical difference. Word lists consisting only of corresponding words in two dialects are often misleading, since differences can be quite subtle and may involve differences in frequency of use, style, or in only one particular sub-sense of a word. We therefore supplement the list with notes.

	AusEng	*EngEng*
1.	*to barrack for*	*to support*
2.	*bludger*	*a loafer, sponger*
3.	*footpath*	*pavement*
4.	*frock*	*dress*
5.	*get*	*fetch*
6.	*goodday*	*hello*
7.	*gumboots*	*wellington boots*
8.	*(one-storey) house*	*bungalow*
9.	*lolly*	*sweet*
10.	*paddock*	*field*
11.	*parka*	*anorak*
12.	*picture theatre*	*cinema*
13.	*radiator*	*(electric) fire*
14.	*sedan*	*saloon car*
15.	*singlet*	*vest*
16.	*station*	*stock farm*
17.	*station wagon*	*estate car*
18.	*stove*	*cooker*
19.	*stroller*	*push-chair*
20.	*wreckers*	*breakers*

Notes

1. *To barrack for* is a term used for support at, for example, football matches and of sports teams: *Who do you barrack for?* The term *to barrack* is known in EngEng but in the meaning of 'shouting abuse or unfavourable comments' at sports teams, and is now somewhat old-fashioned.
2. *Bludger* is colloquial only.
3. In EngEng, *footpath* refers to a path across fields, through woods, etc., while *pavement* refers to a pathway beside a road or street. In AusEng, *footpath* covers both. Both *pavement* and *sidewalk* do occur, however, in certain areas of Australia.
4. Both varieties permit both words. *Frock*, however, sounds old-fashioned in EngEng and is not used in advertising as it is in AusEng.

5. *Get* is widely used in both varieties, but usages such as *I'll fetch it for you* are much less usual in AusEng than in EngEng.
6. *Goodday* [gədei] is a common, colloquial form of greeting in AusEng.
7. *Gumboots* is understood in EngEng but sounds rather archaic. Both varieties also use the term *rubber boots*.
8. EngEng distinguishes between *bungalow* 'a one-storey house' and *house* 'a two or more storey house', although *house* is also a generic term covering both. In Australia (where, in fact, bungalows are a good deal more common than in Britain), this distinction is not made. *Bungalow*, however, is used in AusEng to refer to a less substantial construction such as a summer house, beach bungalow, etc.
9. In EngEng, *lolly* is an abbreviation of *lollipop* (a word of Romany origin), which is a sweet on a stick, designed for licking. In AusEng, *lolly* is a generic term corresponding to EngEng *sweet. Sweet* is used in AusEng, but usually as a rather formal shop-type word.
10. The word *paddock* is used in EngEng with the more restricted meaning of a field that is used for grazing horses. The AusEng usage refers to any piece of fenced-in land. *Field* is used in AusEng with abstract meaning and also in reference to, for example, a *football field* (= EngEng *football pitch*). Many words referring to European-type countryside features, such as *brook, stream, meadow*, are unusual or poetic in AusEng.
11. The word *parka* is known in EngEng but in recent years has been replaced by *anorak*, although some manufacturers may make a distinction, using these terms, between different types of coat. Both words are loans from Eskimo.
12. *Cinema* is in fact used in both varieties, but is rather higher style in AusEng. One doesn't say *picture theatre* in EngEng, but both varieties have the informal phrase *going to the pictures*.
13. *Radiator* is used in EngEng, but only with reference to hot water or oil radiators, e.g. those used in central-heating systems. In EngEng both portable and fixed heaters consisting of electrically heated bars are known as *fires*.
14. Here AusEng follows NAmEng.
15. The garment referred to here is an undershirt. *Singlet* is known and used in EngEng, but *vest* is not usual in AusEng.
16. In AusEng a *station* refers to a large cattle or sheep farm (besides having the meaning common to all forms of English, as in *railway station*).
17. Here AusEng follows NAmEng.
18. *Cooker* is not usual in AusEng, while both *cooker* and *stove* are used in EngEng.
19. *Stroller* is known in EngEng, but is not so widely used as *push-chair*. Some forms of AusEng also use *push-chair* or '*pushy*'.
20. The reference here is to premises dealing with old, broken down, or crashed cars.

Most lexical differences within the English-speaking world can be found at the level of colloquial speech, and especially in that faddish, often transitory form known as 'slang'. AusEng slang or colloquial expressions not known in EngEng include:

to chunder	'to vomit'
crook	'ill, angry'
a dag	'an eccentric person'
a drongo	'a fool'
to rubbish	'to pour scorn on'
a sheila	'a girl'
to front up	'to arrive, present oneself somewhere'
to bot	'to cadge, borrow'
hard yakka	'hard work'
to shoot through	'to leave'
tucker	'food'
a wog	'a germ'
a spell	'a rest, break'
a park	'a parking space'
to shout	'to buy something for someone' (e.g. a round of drinks)
a humpy	'a shelter, hut'
to chyack	'to tease'
an offsider	'a partner, companion'
a chook	'a chicken'
a larrikin	'a young ruffian'
to dob	'to plonk' (something down on something)
to fine up	'to improve' (of weather)
beaut	'very nice, great'
to retrench	'to sack, make redundant'
financial	'paid up' (as of a member of a club)
interstate	'in another' (Australian) state

For a note on AusEng spelling, see 4.2.1.(1).

2.2.1.7. Usage

1. It is usual in AusEng to use *thanks* rather than *please* in requests: *Can I have a cup of tea, thanks?*
2. Colloquial abbreviations are more frequent than in EngEng: e.g. *beaut* 'beautiful, beauty'; *uni* 'university'.
3. Abbreviated nouns ending in -/i:/ are more common in colloquial AusEng than in EngEng, and many forms occur which are known in EngEng: e.g. *truckie* 'truck driver'; *tinnie* 'tin'—used especially of a can of beer.
4. Abbreviated nouns ending in -/ou/ are much more common in colloquial AusEng than in EngEng, and many forms occur which are unknown in EngEng: e.g. *arvo* 'afternoon'; *muso* 'musician'.
5. Abbreviated personal names ending in -/zə/ or /z/ are common, e.g. *Bazza* 'Barry'; *Mezza* 'Mary'; *Shaz* 'Sharon'.

2.2.2. NZEng

English has been spoken in New Zealand since the early nineteenth century and has about 4 million native speakers there.

2.2.2.1. New Zealand vowels

Phonetically and phonologically, NZEng accents are very similar to AusEng, and 'mild' AusEng and NZEng accents are difficult for outsiders to tell apart, particularly in the case of older speakers. NZEng is like AusEng in having /i:/ in *very* etc., and /ə/ in *naked* etc. It also has wider and slower diphthongs than RP, a very front /ɑ:/, and lacks smoothing (see 2.1.1.). The phonetic differences between RP and NZEng vowels are indicated in Table 2.4. The major characteristics of the NZEng vowel system are the following:

1. Phonetically speaking, the NZEng vowel /ɪ/ as in *bid* is a central vowel in the region of [ə]. The contrast between AusEng *bid* [bid] and NZEng [bəd] is very clear, and the most noticeable indication of whether a speaker is an Australian or a New Zealander. As a further, linked development, the vowel /ɪ/ = [ə] has become merged with /ʊ/ after /w/, so that, for example, *women* has become identical in pronunciation to *woman* (see also (7) below). Phonologically, we can say that younger New Zealanders, at least, have no distinction between /ɪ/ and /ə/, and thus pronounce, for example, *finish* [fənəʃ], *Philip* [fələp], as compared to AusEng [filəp] and RP [fɪlɪp]. This means that there is no need to postulate /ə/ as a separate vowel in more recent varieties of NZEng—we recognize only the vowel /ɪ/, pronounced [ə].
2. In one phonological context, the RP vowel /ə/ corresponds not to /ɪ/, as discussed in (1) above, but to /ʌ/. In unstressed word-final position, NZEng has a vowel identical to the stressed vowel of *putt*, e.g. *butter* /bʌtʌ/. Notice that this applies to the indefinite article *a*: *a cup* /ʌ kʌp/.
3. The front vowels /ɛ/ as in *bed* and /æ/ as in *bad* are even closer than in AusEng: *bed* [bẹd], *bad* [bẹd]. In the speech of younger New Zealanders, *bed* may be misinterpeted by outsiders as *bead*, and *bad* as *bed*.
4. For most speakers, as in South Australia, most words in the set of *dance, sample, grant, branch* have /ɑ:/ = [a:] rather than /æ/. A few words in the *laugh* set, however, generally have /æ/. This is especially true of *telegraph, graph*.
5. There is a strong and growing tendency for /ɪə/ and /ɛə/ to merge, so that pairs such as *beer, bear* are pronounced identically: [bẹ:~bẹə]. Beer may be advertised with pictures of bears, and hairdressers pu up signs saying 'Hair it is!'
6. For many speakes, /ɒ/ and /ou/ are merged before /l/, so that *doll* and *dole* are identical. Distinctions between other vowels may also be neutralized before /l/, as well as before /r/, so that *pull* and *pool*, *fellow* and *fallow*, *will* and *wool*, and *Derry, dairy* and *dearie* may be

Table 2.4. Phonetic differences between NZEng and RP vowels

		RP	**NZEng**
bid	/ɪ/	[ɪ]	[ə]
bed	/ɛ/	[ɛ]	[e̞]
bad	/æ/	[æ]	[ɛ̞]
pot	/ɒ/	[ɒ]	[ɒ]
putt	/ʌ/	[ɐ]	[ɐ˗]
put	/ʊ/	[ʊ]	[ɤ]
bee	/iː/	[ɪi]	[ɜ·ɪ]
bay	/ei/	[eɪ]	[a·ɪ]
buy	/ai/	[aɪ]	[ɑ·ɪ]
boy	/ɔi/	[ɔɪ]	[o̞·ɪ]
boot	/uː/	[ʉu]	[ə·ʉ]
boat	/ou/	[əu]	[ɐ̈ʉ~ɐ̈ɵ]
bout	/ɑu/	[ɑu]	[æ·ʉ]
peer	/ɪə/	[ɪə]	[e̞ə]
pair	/ɛə/	[ɛə]	[e̞ə]
paw	/ɔː/	[ɔː]	[ɔ̈]
bard	/ɑː/	[ɑː]	[aː]
bird	/ɜː/	[ɜː]	[ø̞·]

identical. Like in AusEng, /l/ is dark in all positions, and there is also an increasing tendency to lip-rounding and vocalization of /l/, i.e. syllable-final /l/ is either [ɫ̫]or a vowel with a quality around [o], e.g. *bell* [beɫ̫~beo].

7. Unlike AusEng, the vowel /ʊ/ tends to be unrounded, as in many types of EngEng (see 2.1.1.).

8. The /ɜː/ vowel of *bird* has a considerable degree of lip-rounding, as in WEng (see 2.3.1.).

2.2.2.2. NZEng consonants

1. In NZEng, the /ʍ/ of *which* has been strongly maintained, more so even than in RP. However, it is now more or less lost in the speech of younger New Zealanders.

2. Intervocalic /t/ as in *city, better* is variably a voiced flap, as in AusEng.

3. Most forms of NZEng are non-rhotic (see 2.1.3.), with linking and intrusive /r/, but the local accents of the southern area of the South Island, comprising parts of Otago and Southland, are rhotic. The area concerned centres on Invercargill and includes Gore, Tapanui, Winton, Nightcaps and Ohai (see Map 2 on page 33). This phenomenon is known to New Zealanders as the 'Southland burr' and is often ascribed to the influence of settlers from Scotland and Ireland.

4. The word *with* is pronounced /wɪθ/, as in ScotEng, CanEng and some forms of USEng, rather than /wɪð/, as in EngEng.

2.2.2.3. NZEng grammar

1. NZEng resembles AusEng in avoiding *shall, should*; in lacking totally the construction *I'll give it him*; and, in the written language at least, in preferring singular verb agreement as in *The team is playing badly*.
2. Many NZEng speakers also take *shall*-avoidance one stage further than AusEng speakers, in the ScotEng manner (see 5.1.4.), and use constructions such as *Will I close the window?* rather than EngEng *Shall I close the window?* NAmEng *Should I close the window?*
3. Corresponding to EngEng *at the weekend* and NAmEng *on the weekend* many NZEng speakers have *in the weekend*.

2.2.2.4. NZEng lexis

In most respects, NZEng agrees with either AusEng (e.g. *lolly* and many of the other items in 2.2.1.6.) or with EngEng. NZEng usages include:

NZEng	*EngEng*
tramping	'hiking'
to farewell	'to say goodbye to'
to front	'to turn up, appear'
to uplift	'to pick up, collect'
a domain	'a recreation area'
to jack up	'to arrange'
an identity	'a character'
to flat	'to live in a shared flat'

Other more colloquial usages include:

to skite	'to boast'
to wag	'to play truant'
a hoon	'a yob'
a bach (from bachelor)	'a cabin, cottage'
a crib	'a cabin, cottage' (southern South Island only)
a Kiwi	'a New Zealander'
lairy	'loud' (of colours—in some areas only)

2.2.2.5. Maori lexis

The indigenous population of New Zealand are the Maori, whose arrival in New Zealand antedates that of Europeans by several hundred and perhaps as much as a thousand years. There are today about 550,000 Maori in New Zealand—about 14 per cent of the population—and about 135,000 of these are native speakers of Maori, which is a Polynesian language related to Tongan, Samoan, Tahitian, Hawaiian and many others. All Maori speakers, however, can also speak English. Many New Zealand place-names are of Maori origin, e.g. Whangarei, Te Anau. A rather large number of Maori words have found their way into the usage of English speakers in New Zealand, most of them, however, being used solely in connection with Maori culture. The following words—the list is not exhaustive—can be found in New Zealand books and newspapers, without translation into English, indicating that most New Zealanders know what they mean:

Maori/NZEng	EngEng
aroha	'love'
haka	'posture dance'
hui	'assembly'
iwi	'tribe'
kaumatua	'elder'
kaupapa	'plan, rule'
mana	'power, honour'
marae	'meeting ground'
pa	'village'
paepae	'threshold'
pakeha	'white person, New Zealander of European origin'
powhiri	'welcome'
rangatira	'chief'
rangatiratanga	'kingdom'
runanga	'assembly, debate'
tangata	'people'
taniwha	'monster'
tapu	'sacred'
taua	'war'
tauiwi	'foreigner'
umu	'oven'
waka	'canoe'
whare	'house'
whakapapa	'genealogy'
whenua	'land, country'

Of these, the word *mana* is also used in non-Maori contexts. The word *tapu* is essentially the same as the English word *taboo*, which was borrowed into English from Tongan. *Pakeha* and *Maori* are the terms normally used to refer to the two major ethnic groups in the country.

2.2.2.6. Usage

1. As in AusEng, certain abbreviated forms not found in EngEng or NAmEng are common in colloquial speech, e.g. *beaut* 'beautiful, beauty'; *ute* 'utility vehicle, pick-up truck'.
2. As in AusEng, *thanks* can be used where other varieties of English normally have *please*: *Can I have a cup of tea, thanks?*
3. As in AusEng, although the words involved are not in all cases the same, colloquial abbreviations ending in -/ou/ are common: *arvo* 'afternoon'; *smoko* 'break, rest period'.
4. As in AusEng, although the words involved are not in all cases the same, colloquial abbreviations ending in -/i:/ are common: *boatie* 'boating enthusiast'; *postie* 'postman, delivery worker' (also found in ScotEng).

Map No. 2. New Zealand South Island

2.2.3. SAfEng

The population of the Republic of South Africa is about 45 million. The African majority, about 70 per cent of the population, speak Bantu languages such as Zulu, Xhosa, Sotho and Tswana. About 20 per cent of the population speak Afrikaans, a language of European origin related to Dutch; and a small percentage speak languages of Indian origin such as Hindi and Tamil. The surviving indigenous languages of the area, the Khoisan ('Bushman' and 'Hottentot') languages, are in a stronger position in neighbouring Nambia and Botswana than they are in South Africa itself.

English has had significant numbers of speakers in South Africa since the 1820s and is currently spoken natively by about 2 million whites and nearly 1 million 'coloured' (mixed race) and Indian-origin speakers. English is also very widely spoken as a second language. Forms of English which closely resemble SAfEng are also spoken natively in Zimbabwe, as well as by relatively small groups of whites in Namibia, Zambia and Kenya.

In what follows we confine our attention to the English of native speakers in South Africa.

Table 2.5. SAfEng vowels

		RP	SAfEng
bid	/ɪ/	[ɪ]	[ə]
bed	/ɛ/	[ɛ]	[e]
bad	/æ/	[æ]	[ɛ]
pot	/ɒ/	[ɒ]	[ɔ]
putt	/ʌ/	[ɐ]	[ɐ˔]
put	/ʊ/	[ʊ]	[u]
bee	/iː/	[ii]	[iː]
bay	/ei/	[eɪ]	[ɐe]
buy	/ai/	[aɪ]	[ɑ·ə]
boy	/ɔi/	[ɔɪ]	[oe]
boot	/uː/	[ʉu]	[ʉː]
boat	/ou/	[əʊ]	[ʌ˔·ə]
bout	/au/	[aʊ]	[æ·ə]
peer	/ɪə/	[ɪə]	[eː]
pair	/ɛə/	[ɛə]	[eː]
paw	/ɔː/	[ɔː]	[oː]
bard	/ɑː/	[ɑː]	[ɑː]
bird	/ɜː/	[ɜː]	[ø˔ː]

2.2.3.1. SAfEng vowels

Just as with AusNZEng, there is a certain amount of variation in the pronunciation of SAfEng, ranging from RP or near-RP to 'broad' SAfEng.
SAfEng is characterized by the following vocalic phenomena:

1. Like RP and NZEng, SAfEng has /ɑː/ in the *dance* set of words. This dis-
    tinguishes it from most forms of AusEng.
2. The feature which most readily distinguishes between SAfEng and
    AusNZEng is the very back pronunciation of /ɑː/ = [ɑː] in *car, dance,*
    etc., contrasting with AusNZEng front [aː].
3. The SAfEng pronunciation of /ɪ/ is also distinctive in that it has both
    the high front [i] of AusEng and the centralized [ə] of NZEng. In
    SAfEng, however, these two pronunciations constitute allophonic
    variants: [i] occurs before and after the velar consonants /k/, /g/ and
    /ŋ/, before /ʃ/, after /h/, and word-initially; [ə] occurs elsewhere. Thus
    big is [big], but *bit* is [bət].
4. There is an even stronger tendency in SAfEng than in AusEng for
    diphthongs to be monophthongized (see Table 2.5).
5. SAfEng shares with AusNZEng the occurrence of /ə/ in the unstressed
    syllables of *naked, village,* etc.
6. SAfEng also agrees with AusNZEng in having /iː/ in the final syllable
    of *very, many,* etc.

2.2.3.2. SAfEng consonants

1. There is a tendency, possibly as a result of Afrikaans influence, for /p/,
    /t/, /tʃ/, /k/ to be unaspirated: *pin* RP [pʰɪn], SAfEng [pən].

2. As in AusNZEng, there is a tendency for intervocalic /t/, as in *better*, to be a voiced flap [d̬], although this is not so widespread or consistent as in NAmEng.
3. In a number of varieties of SAfEng, the 'dark *l*' [ɫ] allophone of /l/ as in *hill* does not occur (see 2.1.3.(1)).
4. SAfEng is *r*-less, lacking non-prevocalic *r* (except in Afrikaans-influenced English varieties). Very many varieties of SAfEng also lack both intrusive *r* and linking *r* (see 2.1.3.(4)): thus, *four o'clock* [fo:(ʔ)əklɔk], *law and order* [lo:ɲo:də]. SAfEng is alone among the 'English' varieties of English in having this characteristic.

   There is a strong tendency for /r/ to be a flap [ɾ], unlike the friction-less continuant [ɹ] of RP or AusNZEng. (Afrikaans speakers often use a trilled [r].)
5. /tj/, /dj/ often are realized as [tʃ], [dʒ], as in many EngEng varieties: *tune* [tʃʉːn] (cf. AusEng).

2.2.3.3. SAfEng grammar and usage

There appear to be even fewer grammatical differences between SAfEng and EngEng than between AusNZEng and EngEng, especially at the level of educated speech.

1. A common 'broad' SAfEng feature is the use of the all purpose response question *is it?*, invariable for person, tense or auxiliary, which corresponds to the complex series *do they, can't he, shouldn't we, will you*, etc. used in other varieties:

   He's gone to town.—Oh, is it? (=EngEng *Oh, has he?*)

2. In 'broader' varieties of SAfEng it is possible in certain constructions and contexts to delete object noun phrases (NPs) after verbs which must have NPs in other varieties, e.g.:

   Have you got?
   Have you sent?
   Did you put?

3. Complement structures of *adjective + infinitive* occur where other varieties have *adjective + of + participle*:
   This plastic is capable to withstand heat (=This plastic is capable of withstanding heat)
4. Non-negative *no* occurs as an introductory particle:

   How are you?
   No, I'm fine, thanks

   The force of this is often to negate assumptions made in the preceding question or comment.

2.2.3.4. SAfEng lexis

As with AusNZEng, the contact of SAfEng with other languages has had an effect on its vocabulary. Among the better-known borrowings are:

from Zulu:
impi	'African warrior band'
indaba	'conference'

from Afrikaans:
dorp	'village'
kraal	'African village'
sjambok	'whip'
veld	'flat, open country'

Differences within formal English vocabulary are not especially numerous but include:

SAfEng	*EngEng*
bioscope	*cinema*
location	(Black) *ghetto*
reference book	*identity document*
robot	*traffic light*

2.3. Welsh English

English is the sole native language of about 80 per cent of the population of Wales, i.e. about 2.5 million people. Many of these have some competence in Welsh. The remaining 20 per cent, about 0.5 million or so, are bilingual native speakers of Welsh and English.

Until quite recently, in most areas of Wales English was a second language learnt in school (as was the case in the Highlands of Scotland). Although this is no longer true and a majority of people in Wales are now native speakers of English, the effect is that Welsh English, at the level of educated speech and writing, is not much different from that of England, except phonetically and phonologically. There are, of course, distinctly Welsh lexical items and grammatical constructions, often due to the influence of Welsh—we have already noted that Welsh English is a 'shift variety'—but Welsh Standard English cannot be said to be particularly different from EngEng. Most differences are found at the level of more localized dialects (see Wells, 1982, and Hughes *et al.*, 2005).

2.3.1. WEng vowels

The Welsh English vowel system is, with some regional variation, as in Table 2.6 and on the recording.

The principal phonological differences between WEng and RP are the following:

1. *last, dance*, etc. tend to have /æ/ rather than /ɑː/ for most WEng speakers, although /ɑː/ is found for many speakers in some words.

2. Unstressed orthographic *a* tends to be /æ/ rather than /ə/, e.g. *sofa* [so:fa].
3. Unstressed orthographic *o* tends to be /ɒ/ rather than /ə/, e.g. *condemn* /kɒndɛm/.
4. There is no contrast between /ʌ/ and /ə/: *rubber* /rəbə/.
5. There is, in many varieties, an additional contrast, between /ei/ and /ɛi/:

made	/meid/	[me:d]
maid	/mɛid/	[mẹɪd]

    Words with /ɛi/ are typically those spelt with *ai* or *ay*.
6. There is, in many varieties, an additional contrast between /ou/ and /ɔu/:

nose	/nouz/	[no:z]
knows	/nɔuz/	[nọʊz]

7. Many words which have /ɔ:/ in RP have the vowel /ou/ = [o:] in many WEng varieties. Thus:

	RP	**WEng**
so	[səu]	[so:]
soar	[sɔ:]	[so:]

    Note, however, that *port, paw* still have /ɔ:/ in WEng.
8. The vowels /ɪə/, /ʊə/ do not occur in many varieties of WEng. *Fear* is /fi:jə/, *poor* is /pu:wə/. Similarly, *fire* is /faijə/.
9. Words such as *tune, music* have /tɪʊn/, /mɪʊzɪk/ rather than /tju:n/, /mju:zɪk/.

Table 2.6. WEng vowels

/ɪ/	[ɪ]	*bid*
/ɛ/	[ɛ]	*bed*
/æ/	[a]	*bad, pass, above, sofa*
/ɒ/	[ɔ]	*pot, object (v.)*
/ʌ/	[ə]	*putt, famous, rubber*
/ʊ/	[ʊ]	*put*
/i:/	[i:]	*bee*
/ei/	[e:]	*bake*
/aʊ/	[əɪ]	*buy*
/ɔʊ/	[ɔɪ]	*boy*
/u:/	[u:]	*boot*
/ou/	[o:]	*boat, board*
/ɑu/	[əʊ]	*bout*
/ɛə/	[ɛ:]	*pair*
/ɔ:/	[ɔ:]	*sort, paw*
/ɑ:/	[a:]	*bard, calm*
/ɜ:/	[ø:]	*bird*
/ɛi/	[ẹɪ]	*bait*
/ɔu/	[ọʊ]	*blow*

2.3.2. WEng consonants

1. Educated WEng is not rhotic with a few exceptions in the east and far south-west of the country; intrusive and linking /r/ do occur; and /r/ is often a flapped [ɾ].
2. Voiceless plosives tend to be strongly aspirated, and in word-final position are generally released and without glottalization, e.g. *pit* [pʰɪtʰ].
3. /l/ is clear [l] in all positions.
4. There is a strong tendency for intervocalic consonants to be lengthened before unstressed syllables:

   butter   [bətʰ:ə]
   money   [mən:i]

5. The Welsh consonants [ɫ] and /x/ occur in place-names and loanwords from Welsh. /ɫ/ is a voiceless, lateral fricative, and /x/ is a voiceless velar fricative as in Scots *loch* or German *acht*, e.g.:

   Llanberis   /ɫanbérɪs/
   bach   /bɑ:x/ (term of endearment)

2.3.3. Non-systemic pronunciation differences

1. For some WEng speakers, /g/ is absent in the following two words:

	WEng	*RP*
language	/læŋwɛdʒ/	/læŋgwɪdʒ/
longer	/lɒʔə/	/laŋgə/

2. For some WEng speakers, /ʊ/ occurs in both of the following words:

	WEng	*RP*
comb	/kʊm/	/koum/
tooth	/tʊθ/	/tu: θ/

2.3.4. WEng grammar

The following features can be observed in the speech of even some educated WEng speakers but are not usually encountered in written Welsh English:

1. The use of the universal tag question *isn't it?*, invariable for main clause person, tense or auxiliary:

   You're going now, isn't it? (=EngEng *aren't you?*)
   They do a lot of work, isn't it? (=EngEng *don't they?*)

2. The use of *will* for *will be*:

   Is he ready? No, but he will in a minute.

3. The use of predicate object inversion for emphasis:

   WEng   *Coming home tomorrow he is*
   EngEng   *He's coming home tomorrow/It's tomorrow he's coming home*

4. The use of negative *too*:

   WEng   *I can't do that, too*
   EngEng   *I can't do that, either*

5. The use of adjective and adverb reduplication for emphasis:

   WEng   *It was high, high*
   EngEng   *It was very high*

2.3.5. WEng lexis

Surprisingly few Welsh loan-words are used in standard WEng. Common words include:

del	/dɛl/	a term of endearment
eisteddfod	/aistéðvɒd/	a competitive arts festival (This word is known to EngEng speakers, who generally pronounce it /aisteðfəd/.)
llymru	/ɬəmriː/	porridge dish

Different WEng usages of English words found in some parts of Wales include:

delight	'interest'	(e.g. *a delight in languages*)
rise	'get, buy'	(e.g. *I'll rise the drinks*)
tidy	'good, nice'	(e.g. *a tidy car*)

Again, most vocabulary differences are at the level of nonstandard or colloquial usage.

|3|

The pronunciation of North American English

The sociolinguistic situation in the United States and Canada, as far as pronunciation is concerned, is rather different from that of the rest of the English-speaking world. There is more regional variation in NAmEng pronunciation than in AusNZEng and SAfEng, yet there is no universally accepted totally regionless standard pronunciation as in EngEng.

In this chapter we will begin by giving an outline of one USEng accent—an accent employed by some educated white middle-class speakers from the central east-coast region. We will then point to differences between this accent and RP. Next we will discuss regional differences within NAmEng pronunciation, concentrating on varieties of educated speech and omitting mention of most lower-prestige accents.

3.1. North American English vowels

Table 3.1 and the first US speaker on the recording illustrate the vowel system of the USEng accent described above. Note that, to aid comparison, vowel symbols have been chosen which are closest to those used in Chapter 2 for the 'English' type accents rather than those typically used by American writers. Note also that this phonological analysis is not so widely accepted as the analysis of RP vowels given in 2.1.1. In particular, the identification of vowel phonemes before /r/ (especially the vowels of *bird*, *port* and *furry*) is not entirely uncontroversial in view of the considerable allophonic variation before /r/:/i/—*peer* [pɪəɹ]; /ei/—*pair* [pɛəɹ]; /ai/—*fire* [faɪəɹ]; /u/—*tour* [tʊəɹ]; /au/—*tower* [taʊəɹ]; /ɔ/—*port* [pɔəɹt]; /ə/—*bird* [bəːɹd]~[bɹ̩d]. This allophonic variation is particularly clear on the recording, suggesting especially that *port*, *boring*, *pore*, etc., might be better analysed as having /our/ rather than /ɔr/.

Table 3.1. USEng vowel system (Central East Coast)*

/ɪ/	*bid, mirror, wanted*
/ɛ/	*bed, merry*
/æ/	*bad, marry, path, dance, half, banana*
/ɑ/	*pot, bard, father, calm, horrid*
/ʌ/	*putt, hurry*
/ʊ/	*put*
/i/	*bee, very, peer*
/ei/	*bay, pair, Mary*
/ai/	*buy, fire, night, ride*
/ɔi/	*boy*
/u/	*boot, tour*
/ou/	*boat*
/au/	*bout, loud, tower*
/ɔ/	*paw, port, talk, boring, long, pore*
/ə/	*about, sofa, bird, furry, butter*

*The words in Table 3.1 are also used in the recording for USEng (Mid-Western) and CanEng (see page 53).

3.1.1. NAmEng vowels: phonological differences from RP

1. NAmEng agrees with all other English varieties we have discussed in differing from RP by having /i/ rather than /ɪ/ in *very* etc. (However, a number of south-eastern and eastern USA varieties *do* have /ɪ/ here.)

2. The three RP vowels /ɒ/, /æ/ and /ɑ:/ correspond to only two vowels in NAmEng—/ɑ/ and /æ/. This, combined with the phonetic difference between RP /ɒ/ and USEng /ɑ/ and a difference in vowel distribution in many sets of words, makes for a complicated set of correspondences. When this is further combined with a different distribution in word sets of the vowels /ɑ/ and /ɔ/ (NAm): /ɒ/ and /ɔ:/ (RP) and the rhotic/non-rhotic difference, the picture becomes even more complex:

	RP	*USEng*
bad	æ	æ
Datsun	æ	ɑ
Bogota	ɒ	ou
pot	ɒ	ɑ
cough	ɒ	ɔ
long	ɒ	ɔ
paw	ɔ:	ɔ
port	ɔ:	ɔr
bard	ɑ:	ɑr
path	ɑ:	æ
dance	ɑ:	æ
half	ɑ:	æ
banana	ɑ:	æ
father	ɑ:	ɑ

This chart illustrates the following points:

(a) In very many words spelled with *a*, the correspondence is straightforward: in *cat, bad, man*, etc., RP /æ/ = NAmEng /æ/. Similarly, in very many words spelled with *o*, the correspondence is also reliable: in *pot, top, nod*, etc., RP /ɒ/ = NAmEng /ɑ/.

The remaining points are somewhat problematic:

(b) Perhaps because in many varieties of USEng /æ/ tends to be rather closer than in RP (see below), many words felt to be 'foreign' have /ɑ/ in USEng corresponding to the /æ/ in RP. Thus *Milan* is /mɪlǽn/ in RP but may be /mɪlán/ in NAmEng, and *Datsun* in USEng is /dátsn/, as if it were spelled *Dotsun*. This tendency is not entirely uncomplicated, however, as there are some words, e.g. *khaki*, where the reverse correspondence is found, i.e. USEng /kæki/, RP /kɑːkɪ/. (CanEng often has /karki/.)

(c) Probably as a consequence of the fact that NAmEng /ɑ/ in *pot* is an unrounded vowel, 'foreign' words spelled with *o* tend to have /ou/ in NAmEng corresponding to /ɒ/ in EngEng:

	EngEng	*NAmEng*
Bogota	/bɒgətɑː/	/bougətə/
Carlos	/kɑːlɒs/	/karlous/

(d) NAmEng does not have the RP distinction /ɒ/—/ɑː/ *bomb—balm*, and therefore has /ɑ/ not only in the set *pot, top*, but also for many words that have /ɑː/ in RP including *father, calm* (for many speakers), *rather* (for some speakers). Thus *father* rhymes with *bother*, and *bomb* with *balm* are pronounced the same.

(e) While both RP and the variety of NAmEng described here have a different vowel in *cot* than in *caught*—RP /kɒt/, /kɔːt/: NAmEng /kɑt/, /kɔt/—the distribution of words over these vowels differs somewhat. In some cases RP /ɒ/ corresponds to NAm /ɑ/, and RP /ɔ:/ to NAm /ɔ/. But it is also the case that RP /ɒ/ corresponds to NAm /ɔ/ in words having an *o* before *ng* or one of the voiceless fricatives /f/, /θ/, /s/ (cf. 2.1.1.(3)). In some areas this also applies to *o* before *g* as in *dog, fog*. This is illustrated in Table 3.2. Foreign learners may find the distribution of /ɑ/ and /ɔ/ in USEng confusing and hard to learn. They can take comfort, however, from the fact that many NAmEng accents in fact do not distinguish between these two vowels at all (see 3.3. below).

(f) While RP does not distinguish between *gnaw* and *nor*, NAmEng, being rhotic, does. (See *paw, port*, on chart.)

(g) Being rhotic, NAmEng has /r/ in *bard* etc. Note that the lack of the RP /ɒ/—/ɑː/ distinction means that *cod* /kad/ and *card* /kard/ are distinguished only by means of the /r/ (cf. RP *cod* /kɒd/, *card* /kɑːd/), while *starry* and *sorry* are perfect rhymes: USEng /stari/—/sari/, EngEng /stɑːrɪ/—/sɒrɪ/.

(h) In words such as *path, laugh, grass*, where RP has /ɑː/ before /θ/, /f/, /s/, NAmEng has /æ/.

(i) This applies also to RP /ɑː/ before /nt/, /ns/, /ntʃ/, /nd/, /mp/. Thus NAmEng agrees with northern English accents and many types of AusEng in having /æ/ rather than /ɑː/ in *plant, dance, branch, sample*, etc.

(j) NAmEng, in this case unlike northern English accents, also has /æ/ in *half, ban<u>a</u>na, can't*.

3. The rhoticity of NAmEng has the consequence that the following RP vowels (derived historically from vowel + /r/) do not occur in NAmEng:

/ɪə/ in *dear* (=NAm /ir/)
/ɛə/ in *dare* (=Nam /eɪr/)
/ʊə/ in *tour* (=NAm /ur/)
/ɜː/ in *bird* (=NAm /ər/—but see 3.1. above)

The final syllable in *idea*—identical in RP to the /ɪə/ of *peer, dear*—is best regarded as being /i/ + /ə/ in NAmEng.

3.1.2. NAmEng vowels: phonetic differences from RP

Perhaps all vowels in NAmEng are somewhat different from RP vowels. The major differences, however, are:

1. The vowel of *pot* is unrounded [ɑ] in NAmEng, rounded [ɒ] in RP.
2. The vowel /ɔ/ of *paw* in USEng tends to be shorter, more open and less rounded than the equivalent vowel /ɔː/ in RP.

Table 3.2. Word distribution of /ɒ/—/ɑ/ and /ɔː/—/ɔ/

RP /ɒ/	NAmEng /ɑ/	RP /ɔː/	NAmEng /ɔ/
cot	cot		
top	top		
pot	pot		
pond	pond		
	calm		
	father		
	Milan		
		caught	caught
		taught	taught
		launch	launch
		bought	bought
		all	all
		tall	tall
		saw	saw
loss			loss
cross			cross
soft			soft
cough			cough
off			off
cloth			cloth
song			song
long			long
wrong			wrong

3. Very front realizations of /ou/ such as RP [øʉ] are not found in most varieties of NAmEng, a typical NAmEng pronunciation being [oʊ] (but see 3.3.1.1.(4) below).
4. The diphthong /ei/ may be closer in NAmEng, [eɪ] as opposed to RP [e̞ɪ].
5. The first element of /ɑu/ tends to be more front in NAmEng than in RP: NAmEng [aʊ], RP [ɑʊ].

3.2. North American English consonants

1. Glottal reinforcement as found in RP (see 2.1.3.(3b)) is not found in NAmEng. Neither is [ʔ] found as an allophone of /t/ in most NAmEng varieties, except before /n/ *button* [bəʔn̩] or, in New York City and Boston, before /l/: *bottle* [bɑʔl̩]. Final /t/, however, is often unreleased in NAmEng, especially before a following consonant, as in *that man*.
2. The RP allophonic differentiation of /l/: [l] vs. [ɫ] (see 2.1.3.(1)) is either not found or not so strong in NAmEng. In most varieties, /l/ is fairly dark in all positions.
3. Intervocalic /t/, as in *better*, in NAmEng is most normally a vocalic flap [d̥], not unlike the flapped /r/, [ɾ], of ScotEng. In many varieties the result is a neutralization of the distribution between /t/ and /d/ in this position, i.e. *ladder* and *latter* both have [d̥]. While the intervocalic consonants are identical, in some varieties the original distinction is preserved through vowel length, with the vowel before /d/ being longer: *ladder* [læ·d̥ ɹ], *latter* [læd̥ ɹ].

   This flapped [d̥] is consistently used in NAmEng in *latter*, *city*, etc. by most speakers, except in very formal styles, where [t] may occur. In the suffix *-ity*, [d̥] may vary with [t], as in *obscurity*, *electricity*. In *plenty*, *twenty*, etc. [nt] alternates with [n~ n̥ ~nd]. Thus *winner* and *winter* may or may not be identical.
4. As we have noted, NAmEng is rhotic and has /r/ in *bird*, *card*, *car*, etc. (and in the word *colonel* [kɹ̩nɫ]). Phonetically speaking, too, the /r/ is pronounced rather differently from that of RP. Acoustically the impression is one of greater retroflexion (the tip of the tongue is curled back further) than in RP, but in fact many Americans achieve this effect by the humping up of the body of the tongue rather than by actual retroflexion.
5. As in AusEng, many USEng speakers have a strong tendency to reduce /lj/ to /j/ as in *million* /mɪjən/.

3.3. Regional variation in United States English

Our examination of an educated central-eastern variety of USEng (3.1., 3.2.) has established the major differences between NAmEng phonology and that of the EngEng types. We now turn to an examination of some of the major

Map No. 3. Regional varieties of educated North American English

regional variants of educated NAmEng and detail some of their main characteristics. For this purpose, we divide the USA up into three main accent areas: the South, the General American area, and the North-east. As we shall see, most of the differences have to do with vowels rather than consonants.

3.3.1. The South
The area of the USA that Americans refer to as The South is in fact the south-eastern area of the United States. Linguistically, this large area can be divided approximately into two sub-regions: the Lower South and the Inland South.

3.3.1.1. Lower Southern
This area consists of eastern Virginia, eastern North Carolina, eastern South Carolina, northern Florida, southern Alabama, Mississippi, Louisiana and

south-eastern Texas. Note that much of the southernmost part of Florida was settled by English speakers only relatively recently and generally has accents of a mixed type more closely resembling those of the West (see 3.3.2.2.), although the older accent of Key West has some Bahamian or Caribbean features.

While there is very considerable regional variation within this area, the major features of the Lower Southern accent are as follows:

1. As far as rhoticity is concerned, the position is rather complicated, but, to simplify somewhat, we can say that, generally, Lower Southern accents are non-rhotic, i.e. they lack non-prevocalic /r/ in words such as *cart* and *car* (see 2.1.3.). Many coastal Lower Southern accents are so non-rhotic, in fact, that, like SAfEng (2.2.3.2.), they lack linking and intrusive /r/ as well as non-prevocalic /r/. It is probable that the loss of /r/ was the result of this innovation from England being diffused outwards in post-settlement times from major East Coast ports such as Charleston.
2. The vowels /ɪ/, /ɛ/, /æ/ often take a schwa offglide in many stressed monosyllables. At its most extreme, this process of 'breaking', as it is known, can give pronunciations such as *bid* [bɪjəd], *bed* [bejəd], *bad* [bæijəd].
3. The vowel /ai/ is often a monophthong of the type [ɑː], as in *high* [haː]. In some parts of The South, this monophthong only occurs word-finally and before voiced consonants, while a diphthongal variant occurs before voiceless consonants, as in *night time* [naɪt taːm].
4. The /ei/ and /ou/ diphthongs tend to have first elements rather more open than elsewhere in North America. These broad diphthongs thus resemble those of AusNZEng, as well as those of southern England.
5. The vowels /ɪ/ and /ɛ/ are not distinct before a nasal consonant, so that words such as *pin* and *pen* are identical.
6. The verb forms *isn't*, *wasn't* are often pronounced with /d/ rather than /z/:/ɪdnt~ɪdn/. There is an increasing tendency to use /d/ rather than /z/ in the word *business* also.

3.3.1.2. Inland Southern
Inland Southern accents are found in West Virginia, Kentucky, Tennessee, western Virginia, western North Carolina, western South Carolina, northern Georgia, northern Alabama, Arkansas, south-western Missouri, Oklahoma, and most of Texas. They include the Appalachian and Ozark mountain varieties. These accents share with the Lower South most of the features cited under 3.3.1.1. above except that they are typically, if sometimes variably, rhotic. This is presumably because these areas were less susceptible to influence from London as a result of being further away from the East Coast ports.

3.3.1.3. Black varieties
Many Black Americans, wherever they come from in the United States, have accents which closely resemble those of White speakers from the Lower

South, although they are not usually identical. The reason for this is that, until the abolition of slavery in the United States, most Americans of African origin were located in the Southern plantation and slave-owning states. On moving to northern and western areas of the USA, Black speakers naturally took their southern accents with them, and subsequent relatively low levels of contact between Black and White Americans have meant that many originally southern features have been maintained in Black speech. Current research suggests that this social separation is also having the consequence that, in the Northern accent area, Black speakers are by and large not participating in the Northern Cities Chain Shift (see 3.3.2.4. below), and that the innovations cited in section 3.3.2.1. below are also almost entirely confined to White speech. (For more on Black varieties, see 6.4.)

3.3.2. General American

General American is a term which is quite widely used by American linguists to describe those American accents—the majority—which do not have marked regional north-eastern or southern characteristics. There are, however, a number of important regional differences within this accent type, which is hardly surprising in view of the vast geographical area it covers.

3.3.2.1. Central Eastern

The Central Eastern area was the area that we discussed at the beginning of this chapter (3.1., 3.2.). In broad outline, the type of vowel system that we discussed in 3.1. is typical of the modern educated USEng accents that are found in south-eastern New York State, most of New Jersey away from New York City, eastern Pennsylvania, Delaware and Maryland. However, we can add a little detail to our earlier description by noting that the vowel system we described in 3.1. is currently being affected by a number of innovations that are altering its character somewhat. These innovations are most apparent in the accents of urban areas and, naturally enough, in the speech of younger people. They include the following:

1. The vowels /ɛ/, /æ/, /ɑ/ are involved in the *Northern Cities Chain Shift.* For an explanation of this phenomenon, see 3.3.2.4.
2. The vowel /ei/ as in *bay* is becoming an increasingly narrow diphthong, with the first element becoming closer, e.g. [ei] rather than [ɛi]. This change is the exact opposite of the change affecting this diphthong in the south of England and in AusNZSAfEng, where the diphthong is getting wider. It also has the effect of distancing accents which have this innovation from accents in the American South (see 3.3.1.), where wide diphthongs are usual.
3. The vowel /ai/ is undergoing a change such that the allophones that occur before voiceless consonants are increasingly different from those that occur elsewhere (cf. 3.3.1. and 3.4.1.). What is happening is that the first element of the diphthong in these contexts is increasingly

being raised in the direction of [ə], giving pronunciations such as *night time* [nəɪt taɪm].

4. The vowel /u/ as in *boot* is becoming increasingly fronted from [u:] in the direction of [ʉ:] (see also 2.1.1., 2.1.2.).

5. The vowel /ou/ of *boat* is acquiring a fronter first element, although it is not yet as advanced as the [øʉ] that is found in some forms of EngEng RP (see 2.1.1.).

3.3.2.2. Western

This area comprises the western states of Washington, Oregon, California, Nevada, Idaho, Utah, Arizona, Montana, Wyoming, Colorado, Arizona, North Dakota and South Dakota. This is an extremely large area, and of course its accents are by no means uniform. In particular, urban speech can often be distinguished from rural speech, with urban varieties being a good deal more innovating. The innovations cited for the Central Eastern area (3.3.2.1.), for instance, are much in evidence in this area also, but they are much more typical of younger speakers in places such as San Francisco, Los Angeles, Seattle and Denver than they are of older speakers in rural Wyoming or Montana.

The Northern Cities Chain Shift (see 3.3.2.4.) is not found in this area. Otherwise, the vowel phonology of this area is identical to that of the Central Eastern area (3.1., 3.3.2.1.), with the two following exceptions:

1. The vowel /ɔ/ of *caught* is gradually disappearing in that it is increasingly becoming merged with the vowel /ɑ/ of *cot*, so that pairs of words such as *taught* and *tot*, *sought* and *sot* are pronounced the same. In the Western area this is a change which is currently in progress, and the merger is thus more apparent in the speech of younger than of older speakers. In certain other regions of North America, this merger has already been completed (see 3.3.2.3., 3.3.3.1., 3.4.1.).

2. The vowel /æ/ of *bad* is merged with /ɛ/ before an /r/ which comes between two syllables, so that *marry* is identical with *merry* [mɛɹi], and *carry* rhymes with *cherry*. This is true of all the General American accents except Central Eastern and is part of a wider pattern in which, in most General American accents, other vowels are also merged before /r/ in words of more than one syllable:

(a) /i:/ and /ɪ/ may be merged before /r/, so that *mirror* and *nearer* are perfect rhymes.

(b) /ɛ/ and /ei/ may be merged before /r/, so that *merry* and *Mary* are pronounced identically. This means that if an accent also has the *merry–marry* merger, then *merry, Mary* and *marry* are all pronounced the same.

(c) /ʌ/ and /ə/ may be merged before /r/, so that *hurry* and *furry* are perfect rhymes.

(d) /ɑ/ may be replaced by /ɔ/ or /ou/ before /r/, so that *horrid* has the same initial syllable as *hoary*, and *horrible* rhymes with *deplorable*. This is not a total merger, however, since /ɑ/ still occurs in this position in a small number of words such as *borrow, sorrow, sorry*, as well as in loan-words such as *sari*, i.e. *sorry* and *sari* are both pronounced /sɑri/ and do not rhyme with *quarry*, which follows the majority pattern, /kwɔri/.

These mergers can all be heard from the second American speaker on the recording.
We should also note that:

3. Words such as *new, nude, tune, student, duke, due*, which in many other accents of English have /nju-/, /tju-/, /dju-/, lack /j/ in these accents, giving pronunciations such as *tune* /tun/, *duke* /duk/.

3.3.2.3. Midland
The Midland area consists of Nebraska, Kansas, western Iowa, most of Missouri, southern Illinois, southern Indiana, southern Ohio and south-western Pennsylvania. In broad outline, the phonology of this area is identical to that of the Western area (3.3.2.2.), except that the accents of south-western Pennsylvania and eastern Ohio have carried the *cot–caught* merger through to completion. Additionally, however, educated speakers from this area may also retain some features typical of the older rural dialects of the area. Notable among these is the behaviour of the vowels /ɪ/, /ɛ/, /æ/, /ʊ/, /ʌ/, /ɑ/, /ɔ/ where they occur before the fricatives /ʃ/ and /ʒ/:

(a) words such as *fish* may be pronounced with /i/, i.e. /fiʃ/, identical to *fiche*;
(b) word such as *push* may be pronounced with /u/, i.e. /puʃ/, rhyming with *douche*;
(c) words such as *special* may be pronounced with a diphthongal [ei], i.e. /speiʃəl/;
(d) words such as *mash* may be pronounced with a vowel of the type [æɪ], i.e. [mæɪʃ];
(e) words such as *hush* may be pronounced with a vowel of the type [əɪ], i.e. [həɪʃ].

Most noticeable, however, is the fact that words such as *wash* may be pronounced with /ɔr/, i.e. /wɔrʃ/, rhyming with *Porsche*.

3.3.2.4. Northern
This area is focused on the major northern cities of Minneapolis, Chicago, Detroit, Cleveland and Buffalo, and covers Minnesota, Wisconsin, northern Illinois, northern Indiana, northern Ohio, northern Pennsylvania, north-western New York and west Vermont. The accents of this area are in most respects broadly identical to those of the Western area. One major difference, however, is that they are currently undergoing a process of change which American linguists have labelled the *Northern Cities Chain Shift*. This relatively recent set of innovations involves the vowels /ɛ/, /æ/ and /ɑ/ in a series of linked movements in vowel space.

1. /ɑ/ is moving forwards to take up a front vowel position [æ~a] closer to the original position of /æ/. This can lead speakers from other accent areas to misinterpret, say, *John* as *Jan*.
2. /æ/ is, in its turn, lengthening and moving upwards through [ɛ:] to [e:] and even diphthongizing to [eə] or [ɪə]. This can lead, at its most advanced, to speakers from other areas misinterpreting, say, *Ann* as *Ian*. The degree of raising and diphthongizing of this vowel varies considerably from place to place, word to word, and phonological environment to phonological environment, with the following consonant being the most important determining factor: e.g. *man* may be [mɪən] but *mat* [mɛət]. Buffalo in New York State is said to be the place where this particular change is at its most advanced.
3. /ɛ/, presumably in order to move out of the way of /æ/ as it rises, is retracting and becoming a more central vowel closer in quality to /ʌ/, so that *best* may sound very like *bust*.

3.3.3. Northeastern

This accent area can be divided into two major subdivisions: Eastern New England and New York City.

3.3.3.1. Eastern New England

A very distinct accent, instantly recognizable to other Americans, is associated with the Eastern New England area. This region centres on the city of Boston and includes the states of Maine, New Hampshire, Rhode Island, eastern Vermont, eastern Connecticut and eastern and central Massachusetts. This accent resembles the accents of England more than any other American accent, and there are a number of phonetic similarities with AusNZEng. This resemblance is due to continuing close links between the port of Boston and London in post-settlement times and the resultant importation of originally southern English features into this area of the United States.

Features of Eastern New England speech which distinguish it from Central Eastern (3.1., 3.3.2.1.) and which are due to historical influences from EngEng include the following:

1. The accents of the area are non-rhotic and have both linking and intrusive /r/ (see 2.1.3.). They share with EngEng and the Southern Hemisphere varieties the vowels /ɪə/, /ɛə/, /ʊə/, /ɜ:/ of *peer, pair, poor, bird*. In regions further away from Boston, however, /r/ does occur after /ə/ in items such as *bird* and *butter*. In the speech of younger speakers, moreover, non-prevocalic /r/ is beginning to be reintroduced as a result of influence from the mainstream American norm.
2. Like EngEng, these accents have an additional vowel /a:/, which is used in words such as *bard*, as well as in words such as *calm* and *father* and words such as *dance* and *path*. This vowel is phonetically a rather front [a:]. This feature, too, is rather recessive, with younger speakers increasingly favouring mainstream American forms.

3. The vowel of *pot, horrid,* etc. is a rounded vowel /ɒ/ rather than the more usual American unrounded /ɑ/.

The other distinctive Eastern New England feature is:

4. The *cot–caught* merger has been completed in these accents, both sets of words having /ɒ/ (see 3.3.2.2.). Because /ɔ/ is lacking, and because these accents are also non-rhotic, items such as *port* also have the /ɒ/ vowel, so that *sot, sought* and *sort* can all be pronounced the same, which is not true of any EngEng accent.
5. Younger speakers in Boston and other urban areas also have the Northern Cities Chain Shift (see 3.3.2.4.).

3.3.3.2. New York City

New York is the largest city in the United States. It too has a very distinctive accent, which is also found in the immediately adjoining areas of New York State, Connecticut and New Jersey. This distinctiveness can be ascribed in part, like that of the Boston area, to the city's role as a port with close links with England at earlier periods, but it is also due in part to considerable immigration by speakers of Yiddish, Irish, Irish English, Italian and other European languages, as well as to independent developments. Sociolinguistically, there is more social stratification on the British model in the accents of New York City than anywhere else in North America, with upper social class accents having many fewer local features than lower class accents. Characteristic features of New York English pronunciation include the following:

1. New York City English, like that of Boston, is non-rhotic, and linking and intrusive /r/ are usual. As a consequence, the local accent shares with RP and the other non-rhotic accents the vowels /ɪə/, /ɛə/, /ʊə/, /ɜː/ as in *peer, pair, poor, bird.* However, as in the Boston area, younger speakers are now becoming increasingly rhotic, especially among higher social class groups.
2. Like Boston, New York also has an additional vowel corresponding to RP /aː/. In New York, however, it is phonetically /ɑə/. This vowel occurs in words such as *bard* as well as in *calm, father,* as in Boston; but unlike Boston, it does not occur in *dance, path,* which have /æ/ instead.
3. The vowel /ɜː/ has a typical New York pronunciation where it occurs before a consonant in the same word, as in *bird, girl.* This is a diphthong of the type [ɜɪ]: [bɜɪd]. This was formerly a pronunciation used by all New Yorkers, but it is now most usual in lower class speech, and is not so frequent in the speech of younger people. In word-final position, as in *her,* [ɜː] occurs.
4. Unlike the Eastern New England accent, words such as *pot, horrid* have the more usual American unrounded vowel /ɑ/.
5. Unlike the Eastern New England accent, the New York accent does not lack the vowel /ɔ/, and so *cot* and *caught* are distinct, and *sot* /sɑt/ is distinct from *sought* and *sort* /sɔt/. The /ɔ/ vowel of *caught, sought, talk, paw, long, off, port, sort,* etc., however, has a distinctive New York

pronunciation which is typically a rather close and often diphthongized vowel of the type [oə] or even [ʊə], as in *off* [ʊəf].

6. The distinctively New York /ai/ vowel of *buy*, *night*, *ride* has a back first element, not unlike that of Cockney or AusNZEng, of the type [ɑɪ] or even [ɒɪ].

7. Many New Yorkers have pronunciations of /θ/ and /ð/ as dental stops [t] and [d]. In the case of /ð/, this can lead to a merger with /d/, so that *then* and *den* are possible homophones. This feature, however, is not so common in educated speech.

8. The accents of New York City are also involved in the Northern Cities Chain Shift (see 3.3.2.4.).

3.4. The pronunciation of Canadian English

As far as phonology is concerned, Canadian English can be divided into three main types: General, Maritime and Newfoundland.

3.4.1. General Canadian

This area covers most of English-speaking Canada, from Victoria and Vancouver in the west to Toronto, Ottawa and the English-speaking minority in Montreal in the east. The vowel system of this type of CanEng is identical with that of the Western area of the United States, although it does not have any of the innovations listed under 3.3.2.1., but with the following additional features:

1. The most distinctive feature of Canadian English, and the one which Americans use in spotting Canadian speakers, is the phenomenon known to linguists as *Canadian Raising*. This refers to the fact that, before voiceless consonants, the diphthongs /ai/ and /au/ have allophones with raised central first elements which differ considerably from those which they have elsewhere. This gives pronunciations such as *night time* [nəɪt taɪm] and *out loud* [əʊt laʊd]. As we saw in section 3.3.2.1., raised variants of /ai/ before voiceless consonants are now becoming common in USEng also, so that it is the raised allophone of /au/ in words such as *out*, *house*, *mouth* which is now the most distinctively Canadian feature. Canadian Raising can be heard on the recording in *night*, *bout*, *about*.

2. The loss of the vowel /ɔ/ and the merger of words such as *cot* and *caught* as /kɑt/ (see also 3.3.2.1., 3.3.2.3., 3.3.3.1.) is complete in all forms of General Canadian English.

3. Unlike General American, Canadian English has /ou/ in words such as *borrow*, *sorrow*, *sorry*. *Sorry* thus rhymes with *hoary*. Loan-words such as *sari* have /ɑ/.

4. The diphthongs /ei/ and /ou/ of *bay* and *boat* are very narrow. (The narrow pronunciation of /ei/ is a well-established feature of CanEng and not an innovation, as it is in some forms of USEng—see 3.3.2.1.)

5. Although American cities such as Detroit and Buffalo are only a short distance from the Canadian border, the Northern Cities Chain Shift (see 3.3.2.4.) is not found in CanEng. Indeed, the vowel /æ/ of *bad* and *bat* may be very open, in some cases approaching [a]. Note too that some foreign words spelt with *a*, such as *pasta*, are pronounced with /æ/, as in EngEng, rather than /ɑ/, as in USEng.

3.4.2. Maritime

The linguistic history of the three Canadian maritime provinces is very different from that of rest of Canada. In the seventeenth and eighteenth centuries Nova Scotia was the site of a struggle for power between England and France. Halifax, Nova Scotia, was founded by the British in 1749. In the 1750s the French 'Acadian' settlers were expelled, and new immigrants arrived from the British Isles and New England. Gaelic-speaking Scottish Highlanders settled in a number of areas of Cape Breton Island, where some Gaelic is still spoken to this day. After the American War of Independence about 35,000 American loyalists arrived and by 1800 New Englanders formed about half of the population. Later, Irish people arrived via Newfoundland or directly from Ireland and settled in and near Halifax.

The British occupied Prince Edward Island in 1758, expelling most of the French-speaking settlers, though some francophone areas still remain. The island was formally ceded to Britain in 1763. More than three-quarters of the population are descendants of early settlers from the British Isles: Highland Scots, Ulster Scots, English and southern Irish, but as in Nova Scotia, there are also descendants of American Loyalists who arrived after the American War of Independence.

The British took over New Brunswick in 1713 and in 1755 expelled large numbers of the French-speaking Acadian settlers, many of whom went to Louisiana. The first English-speaking settlers came north from New England in 1762. There was then a big influx of 14,000 Loyalist Americans after the War of Independence, who came mostly from the New York area. The English-speaking majority today—about two-thirds of the population—thus consists largely of descendants of American Loyalists, together with the descendants of Scottish, Irish, and English settlers who arrived in the 1700s and 1800s. The province is today officially bilingual, and some places, notably the town of Moncton, are inhabited by people who are also very much bilingual.

The English of younger educated speakers in some urban areas of the Maritimes such as Halifax is not radically different from that of the rest of Canada. But in many places, especially rural areas, Maritime English is distinctively different, having a number of similarities with the English of Newfoundland, and phonological features which appear to owe much to Irish or Scottish (including Scottish Gaelic) influence, such as affricated word-final /t/ (see 5.2.4.). Canadian Raising is not generally found in rural speech.

3.4.3. Newfoundland

The island of Newfoundland has been part of Canada only since 1949. The population is about 550,000. About 95 per cent of these are of British and Irish origin, whereas fewer than 3 per cent are of French extraction. Most rural areas are inhabited either by people whose ancestors came as early settlers from Dorset and Devon or by people with (rather later) origins in south-eastern Ireland.

The history of the settlement of Newfoundland goes a long way to explaining the current linguistic situation there. The phonology of modern Newfoundland English is characterized by considerable social variation by North American standards, and nonstandard grammatical forms, such as present-tense -s for all persons, occur very frequently and high up the social scale. There is also considerable regional variation. A first impression for English English speakers is that speakers 'sound Irish', but closer listening shows that this is not entirely so. Overall, varieties seem to be the result of a mixture of southern Irish English and south-western English English varieties, but in different proportions in different places. The capital, St Johns, is particularly heavily Irish influenced. It is also one of the few places in North America where it can be said that conservative Traditional Dialects survive. In communities where immigration from Dorset and Devon played an important role, older speakers may still have the initial-fricative voicing in *fish* [vɪʃ], *seven* [zɛvən] typical of the older dialects of the south-west of England; and a number of Irish-origin syntactic features can be found in Irish-influenced areas, such as habitual aspect expressed by *do be* as in *They do be full* 'they are usually full'. For many speakers, the vowels of *cot* and *caught* remain distinct, unlike in mainland Canada. And Canadian Raising is generally not found either. In fact, many speakers have central onsets in /ai/ and /au/ in all phonological environments, e.g. *night time* [nəɪt təɪm], *out loud* [əʊt ləʊd].

3.5. Non-systematic differences between North American English and English English pronunciation

Many of the differences between 'American' and 'English' varieties of English involve the pronunciation of individual or small groups of words. We now give some indication of these.

1. We list first a few individual words which differ in no particularly predictable way between USEng and EngEng (note that CanEng often uses the EngEng variant; stress is the same for both pronunciations of these words):

	USEng	**EngEng**
charade	/ʃəreɪd/	/ʃərɑːd/
cordial	/kɔrdʒəl/	/kɔːdiːəl/
deterrent	/dɪtərənt/	/dɪterənt/

herb	/ərb/	/hɜːb/
leisure	/liʒər/	/lɛʒə/ (also US)
lever	/lɛvər/	/liːvə/ (also US)
privacy	/praivəsi/	/prɪvəsɪ/~/praivəsɪ/
route	/rut/~/raut/	/ruːt/
schedule	/skɛdʒəl/	/ʃɛdʒuːl/
shone	/ʃoun/	/ʃɒn/
tomato	/təmeitou/	/təmɑːtou/
vase	/veis/~/veiz/	/vɑːz/

2. NAmEng *aluminum* /əlúmənəm/ differs both in pronunciation and (as a reflection of this) in spelling from EngEng *aluminium* /æ̀luːmínjəm/.
3. *Either, neither* can have either /iː/:/i/ or /ai/ on both sides of the Atlantic, but in educated speech /iðər/ is more common in USEng, /aiðə/ in EngEng.
4. A number of words spelled with *er* have /ər/ in NAmEng corresponding to /ɑː/~/ar/ elsewhere: *clerk,* NAmEng /klərk/, EngEng /klɑːk/. Similarly *derby, Berkshire.*
5. *Of, what, was* have /ʌ/ in NAmEng, /ɒ/ elsewhere. Thus *what* rhymes with *but* in NAmEng but with *not* in EngEng.
6. *Apparatus, data, status* can be pronounced with either stressed /æ/ or /ei/ in NAmEng, but only with stressed /ei/ in EngEng.
7. Words like *fertile, hostile, juvenile, missile, mobile, sterile* have final /ail/ in EngEng. In NAmEng, the final syllable may be either /ail/ or /əl/. Note that *docile* is /dousail/ in EngEng, /dɑsəl/ in NAmEng.
8. The prefixes *anti-* and *semi-* have final /ɪ/~/iː/ in EngEng. In addition to these pronunciations, NAmEng also has final /ai/ for these prefixes.
9. *Tunisia* is pronounced /tuníʒə/ in NAmEng but /tjuːnízi:ə/ in EngEng. *Asia* has /ʒ/ in NAmEng, /ʃ/ or /ʒ/ in EngEng.

3.6. Stress differences

1. In a number of words of foreign, especially French, origin, NAmEng tends to have stress on the final syllable while EngEng does not. Thus:

	NAmEng	**EngEng**
attaché	/ætæʃéi/	/ətǽʃei/
ballet	/bæléi/	/bǽlei/
baton	/bət án/	/bǽtɒn/
beret	/bəréi/	/bérɪ/~/bérei/
debris	/dəbrí/	/débriː/

2. There are a number of words having first-syllable stress in NAmEng but with stress elsewhere in EngEng. A few examples are:

	NAmEng	**EngEng**
address	/ǽdres/~/ədrés/	/ədrés/
adult	/ǽdʌlt/~/ǽdəlt/	/ədʌ́lt/~/ǽdʌlt/

cigarette	/síɡərɛt/~/sɪɡərét/	/sɪɡərét/
inquiry	/íŋkwərɪ/~/ɪŋkwáɪrɪ/	/ɪŋkwáɪərɪ/
magazine	/mǽɡəzin/~/mæɡəzín/	/mǽɡəzíːn/
margarine	/márdʒərən/	/mɑːdʒəríːn/
research	/rísərtʃ/	/rəséːtʃ/

Note that *research*, as a noun, is now increasingly pronounced with first-syllable stress in EngEng.

3. A number of compound words have acquired stress on the first element of NAmEng but retain stress on the second element in EngEng. The compounds include *weekend*, *hotdog*, *New Year*, *ice cream*.

4. Many polysyllabic words ending in *-ory* or *-ary* normally have stress on the first or second syllable in EngEng, with the penultimate syllable being reduced. In NAmEng there is, in addition, secondary stress on the penultimate syllable:

	NAmEng	**EngEng**
auditory	/ɔ́dɪtɔ̀ri/	/ɔ́ːdɪtrɪ/
commentary	/káməntɛ̀ri/	/kɒ́məntrɪ/
dictionary	/díkʃənɛ̀ri/	/díkʃənrɪ/
lavatory	/lǽvətɔ̀ri/	/lǽvətrɪ/
secretary	/sékrətɛ̀ri/	/sékrətrɪ/

In EngEng, partially reduced pronunciations are also possible, but there is never secondary stress on the penultimate syllable: *dictionary* /díkʃənərɪ/.

In a number of words of this set, the primary stress is also located differently:

	USEng	**EngEng**
laboratory	/lǽbrətɔ́ri/	/ləbɒ́rətrɪ/
corollary	/kárəlɛ̀ri/	/kərɒ́lərɪ/
capillary	/kǽpɪlɛ̀ri/	/kəpílərɪ/
ancillary	/ǽnsɪlɛ̀ri/	/ænsílərɪ/

(Note that all words discussed here have at least four syllables in NAmEng: i.e. none of the above remarks applies to, e.g. *vagary*.)

The same type of difference also appears in a number of words ending in *-mony*:

	NAmEng	**EngEng**
matrimony	/mǽtrɪmòuni/	/mǽtrɪmənɪ/
testimony	/téstɪmòuni/	/téstɪmənɪ/

5. Many place names (and family names derived from them) demonstrate more stress and vowel reduction in EngEng than in NAmEng:

	NAmEng	**EngEng**
Birmingham	/bɜ́rmɪŋhæ̀m/	/bɜ́ːmɪŋəm/
Cunningham	/kʌ́nɪŋhæ̀m/	/kʌ́nɪŋəm/
Norfolk	/nɔ́rfouk/	/nɔ́ːfək/
Norwich	/nɔ́rwɪtʃ/	/nɒ́rɪdʒ/
Portsmouth	/pɔ́rtsmòuθ/	/pɔ́ːtsməθ/

3.7. Further differences between American English and Canadian English pronunciation

In a few respects, Canadian pronunciation follows EngEng rather than USEng:

1. *been* is usually /bɪn/ in USEng, but occasionally /biːn/ in CanEng as, more usually, in EngEng.
2. *again(st)* is usually /əgén/ in USEng. This pronunciation is also used in Canada and the UK, but in CanEng and EngEng it can also be /əgeín/.
3. As mentioned above, *corollary*, *capillary* are stressed on the first syllable in USEng, with secondary stress on the penultimate syllable. CanEng follows EngEng in having the stress on the second syllable.
4. CanEng has *shone* as /ʃan/, never /ʃoun/ as in USEng.
5. Some CanEng speakers have *tomato* as /təmætou/.

|4|

English and North American English: grammatical, orthographical and lexical differences

At the level of educated speech and writing, there are relatively few differences in grammar and spelling between EngEng and NAmEng; those which do exist tend to be fairly trivial when considered from the point of view of mutual understanding. Vocabulary differences, on the other hand, are very numerous and are capable of causing varying degrees of comprehension problems. Each of these three areas will be discussed in turn below.

It should be noted that we treat EngEng and NAmEng, often, as if they were two entirely homogeneous and separate varieties. This makes the presentation of the facts more straightforward, but it does obscure, to a certain extent, the fact that there is regional variation, even in Standard English, in the two areas. There is also considerable influence of the one variety on the other, particularly of NAmEng on EngEng; thus, what is NAmEng usage for older English people may be perfectly normal EngEng usage for younger English people.

4.1. Grammatical differences

In this section we will discuss differences both in morphology and syntax. We will also note some differences in frequency of use of certain constructions which occur in both varieties.

4.1.1. The verb

4.1.1.1. Morphology

1. *Inflectional.* In English, 'regular' verbs are characterized as having two distinct 'principal parts': a present tense form, and a past tense/past participle form which is made by adding -*(e)d* to the present tense form, e.g.:

Present	Past	Past Participle
call	called	called
create	created	created

There are many 'irregular' or 'strong' verbs in English, however, which do not follow this pattern, diverging in a variety of ways, e.g.:

Present	Past	Past Participle
fly	flew	flown
hit	hit	hit
sing	sang	sung
teach	taught	taught

In NAmEng, a number of irregular verbs have become regularized, while remaining irregular in EngEng:

(a) In many instances, it is only the voicing of the past tense morpheme -*(e)d* which has been changed to regularize the verb:

	EngEng	
Present	Past and Past Participle	Past and Past Participle
burn	burnt	burned
dwell	dwelt	dwelled
learn	learnt	learned
smell	smelt	smelled
spell	spelt	spelled
spill	spilt	spilled
spoil	spoilt	spoiled

(b) In some irregular EngEng verbs, there is a vowel change from /i/ in the present to /ɛ/ in the past and past participle forms. The NAmEng forms retain the present tense vowel in the following cases, as well as voicing the ending:

	EngEng	USEng
Present	Past and Past Participle	Past and Past Participle
dream	dreamt /drɛmt/	dreamed /drimd/
kneel	knelt	kneeled
lean	leant	leaned
leap	leapt	leaped

The NAmEng forms are also possible now in EngEng and the EngEng forms may still be found in formal language and poetry in NAmEng.

(c) In a few instances, the NAmEng forms are more irregular than the EngEng forms:

	EngEng	*NAmEng*	
Present	*Past and Past Participle*	*Past*	*Past Participle*
dive	dived	dove	dived
fit	fitted	fit	fitted
sneak	sneaked	snuck	snuck
get	got	got	gotten

NAmEng also uses *dived*, *fitted*, and *sneaked* for the past tense, but the irregular forms are more frequent:

He dove/dived in head first
That suit fit/fitted me last week
He snuck/sneaked around the corner

The past participle *gotten* is not used in EngEng. In NAmEng it was formerly restricted to being used in the sense of 'obtain' or 'acquire':

I've gotten a new car since I last saw you

Now, however, *gotten* can be used in all meanings except for 'have' in NAmEng, e.g.:

We have gotten home late again
We've gotten together every June
We had already gotten off the train when it was hit
They've gotten me into trouble again

but

I've got plenty to eat
I've got the idea now (= 'I understand')

2. *Derivational*
(a) One way of making or 'deriving' new verbs is to add a verb-forming suffix or prefix onto a noun or adjective: e.g. *symbol—symbolize, ripe—ripen, frost—defrost*. While it is usually the case that the same derivational suffixes are productive in both varieties of English, NAmEng tends perhaps to be more productive in its derivations, i.e. some affixes are used on classes of words or with particular senses of words where they would not be used in EngEng. While many such derived words are considered 'jargon' and not accepted into common use in NAmEng, those which are accepted are often borrowed quickly into EngEng.

Two verb-forming affixes which are somewhat more productive in USEng than EngEng are:

-ify: *citify, humidify, uglify*
-ize: *burglarize, decimalize, hospitalize, rubberize, slenderize*

(b) Another way of forming new words is by simply changing a word's grammatical class, e.g. using a noun as a verb. This process is common to both varieties, with innovations spreading rapidly from one to the other. Again, there is more of a tendency to form new words in this way in USEng than in EngEng, e.g.:

Noun	*Verb*
an author	*to author*
a host	*to host (e.g. We hosted a reunion last week)*
a sky-rocket	*to sky-rocket (e.g. Prices are sky-rocketing this year)*
pressure	*to pressure (EngEng to pressurize)*
a room	*to room (e.g. I room at that house)*

4.1.1.2. Auxiliaries

An auxiliary verb, as the name implies, does not exist as an independent verb in a sentence but must combine with a lexical verb to form a verb phrase. Different auxiliaries have various functions, such as entering into specific syntactic processes (question formation, negative contraction), expressing aspect (progressive and perfective), and expressing modality (volition, probability, obligation).

1. *Modal auxiliaries*. Several of the modals are used with a different frequency or meaning in NAmEng than in EngEng:

(a) *shall*. *Shall* is rarely used in NAmEng, except in legal documents or very formal styles, and is replaced by *will* (or *should* in questions with first person subjects). The negative form *shan't* is even rarer in USEng. Both varieties also often use the contracted form *'ll*.

EngEng	*NAmEng and EngEng*
I shall tell you later	*I will tell you later/I'll tell you later*
Shall I drink this now?	*Should I drink this now?*
I shan't be able to come	*I won't be able to come*

(b) *should*. As well as expressing obligation and tentativeness, *should* in EngEng can also have a hypothetical sense when it occurs in a main clause with a first person subject followed by a conditional clause. This use is mainly restricted to older speakers and writers. In NAmEng (and with younger EngEng speakers), *would* is used instead in such sentences:

(Older) EngEng   *I should enjoy living here if I could afford to do so*

NAmEng and younger EngEng *I would enjoy living here if. . .*

(c) *would*. USEng has two uses for this modal that are much less usual in EngEng. First, *would* can be used in expressing a characteristic or habitual activity in USEng:

When I was young, I would go there every day

In EngEng either the simple past or the verb with the modal *used to* would probably be used (this is also possible in USEng):

When I was young, I $\begin{Bmatrix} \textit{went} \\ \textit{used to go} \end{Bmatrix}$ *there every day*

Second, while in EngEng *would* cannot be used to express a hypothetical state if this is already signalled by the verb or by a conditional clause, in many USEng dialects *would* can be used in this way in informal speech:

USEng only	**EngEng and USEng**
I wish I would have done it	*I wish I had done it*
If I would have seen one, I would	*If I had seen one, I would have*
have bought it for you	*bought it for you*

(This second use of *would* is relatively recent in USEng and is more likely to be encountered in speech than in writing.)

In EngEng, *would* and *will* are often used in a predictive sense, as in:

That will be the postman at the door
That would be the building you want
Would that be High Street over there?

In USEng, it is more common to use the auxiliaries *should* or *must* in such sentences or not to have any auxiliary:

That $\begin{Bmatrix} \textit{is} \\ \textit{should be} \\ \textit{must be} \end{Bmatrix}$ *the mailman at the door*

That $\begin{Bmatrix} \textit{is} \\ \textit{should be} \end{Bmatrix}$ *the building you want*

Is that High Street over there?

These other forms are also used in EngEng.

(d) *must.* The negative of epistemic *must* is *can't* in southern EngEng:

He must be in—his TV is on
He can't be in—his car has gone

(In the north-west of England, *mustn't* is used rather than *can't*.)

In USEng, the most common negative of epistemic *must* is *must not*. Note that, unlike north-west-EngEng, in USEng this cannot be contracted to *mustn't* without changing the meaning of the auxiliary to 'not be allowed':

He must not be in—his car is gone   (epistemic)
You mustn't be in when we arrive   ('not allowed')

However, *mustn't* can be epistemic in the past perfect:

He mustn't have been in

Even in such cases, however, the uncontracted form is preferred in USEng.

(e) *use(d) to.* In questioning or negating sentences with the modal *used to,* EngEng can treat *used to* either as an auxiliary, in which case it inverts in questions and receives negation, or as a lexical verb requiring *do* for these constructions:

He used to go there
Used he to go there?   (auxiliary)
Did he use to go there?   (lexical verb)
He used not to go there   (auxiliary)
He didn't use to go there   (lexical verb)

In USEng, *used to* is treated only as a lexical verb in these constructions, and this is also becoming increasingly the case in EngEng.

(f) *ought to.* USEng rarely uses this auxiliary in questions or negated forms. Instead, *should* is used:

EngEng   **USEng**
Ought we to eat that?   *Should we eat that?*
(older speakers)

You $\left\{ \begin{array}{l} \textit{ought not} \\ \textit{oughtn't} \end{array} \right\}$ *to have said that*   *You shouldn't have said that*
                                    You oughtn't have said that
                                    (rare, formal)

Note that when *ought* is used in USEng in the negative, the *to* is usually deleted.

EngEng also can treat *ought to* as a lexical verb, similar to *used to,* in informal styles. These forms are considered nonstandard in USEng:

Did you ought to eat that?
You didn't ought to have said that

(g) *dare* and *need.* Both of these auxiliaries are rare in USEng and usually occur in set phrases, such as:

Need I say more?
Persons under 18 need not apply
I dare say . . .

As with *used to,* USEng treats *dare* and *need* as lexical verbs in negating and questioning. EngEng also has this option:

$\left\{ \begin{array}{l} \text{EngEng (only):} \\ \text{USENG and} \\ \text{EngEng:} \end{array} \right.$ *Need you be so rude?*   (auxiliary)

                                    Do you need to be so rude?   (verb)

$\left\{ \begin{array}{l} \text{EngEng (only):} \\ \text{USEng and} \\ \text{EngEng:} \end{array} \right.$ *You needn't be so rude!*   (auxiliary)

                                    You don't need to be so rude! (verb)

EngEng (only):	*Dare I tell the truth?*	(auxiliary)
USEng and		
EngEng:	*Do I dare (to) tell the truth?*	(verb)

EngEng (only):	*I daren't tell the truth*	(auxiliary)
USEng and		
EngEng:	*I don't dare (to) tell the truth*	(verb)

(h) *mayn't*. The contracted form of *may not* is only found in EngEng, and fairly rarely even there.

2. *do*. The auxiliary *do*, which is empty of meaning, is required in all varieties when constructing question and negative forms of simple verbs. (*Do you want this? I don't want this.*) It can also be used for polite commands or requests: *Do go on! Do sit down.* This last use is much less common in USEng, where *please* would be used instead.

3. The verb *to have* in modern English can function either as an auxiliary verb, like the modals, or as a main verb, like the full verbs. Auxiliary verbs in English function as 'operators' which do not require *do*-support and are employed in negation, interrogation, ellipsis and emphasis. They also have phonologically reduced forms, and can co-occur with other reduced forms such as *'s* and *n't*:

I will not go
Will you go?
Yes, I will
I WILL go
I'll go
I won't go

Full verbs, on the other hand, require *do*-support in interrogation, negation and emphasis; have no function is ellipsis; have no reduced forms; and cannot co-occur with other reduced forms:

I do not swim
Do you swim?
Yes, I do
I DO swim
*I swim not
*Swim you?
Yes, I swim
*I swimn't

We might therefore expect to see this pattern occurring also in the case of the two *haves*, with auxiliary *have* behaving like *will* and main verb *have* behaving like *swim*. And indeed we do see precisely this pattern in NAmEng:

Auxiliary
I have not seen him
Have you seen him?

Yes, I have
I HAVE seen him
I've seen him
He's seen him
He hasn't seen him

Main verb

I don't have a good time there
Do you have a good time there?
No, I don't
I DON'T have a good time there

EngEng, on the other hand, does not work like this. Traditionally, EngEng has distinguished between the grammatical behaviour of main verb *have* in dynamic senses such as 'receive', 'take', 'experience', which behaves like a full verb, as in NAmEng:

Do you have coffee with breakfast?
Yes, I do
I don't have coffee with breakfast
I DO have coffee with breakfast

and stative *have*, where the meaning indicates an ongoing state involving possession, where, unlike in NAmEng, *have* does not require *do*-support:

Have you (any) coffee in the cupboard?
I haven't (any) coffee in the cupboard
I HAVE some coffee in the cupboard
I've some coffee in the cupboard

In traditional EngEng, that is, *Do you have coffee in the cupboard?* could only imply the rather unusual activity of drinking coffee in cupboards. Nowadays, however, and especially in the south of England, the stative forms with *do*-support typical of NAmEng are beginning to be used in EngEng also.

In all forms of English, stative *have* can be replaced by *have got*, although this is more common in British than in American English.

4. In NAmEng, uninverted response questions of the type:

John went home
He did?

I'll do it
You will?

are very common, and indicate only mild surprise or interest. In EngEng inverted response questions such as:

John went home
Did he?

I'll do it
Will you?

are really the only possibility, although the NAmEng forms may be possible for some EngEng speakers as an indication of strong surprise.

4.1.1.3. Verb phrase substitutions with *do*

In both EngEng and NAmEng, lexically empty *do* can substitute for a simple finite verb phrase which is the repetition of a verb phrase from the same or preceding sentence. *Do* is inflected for tense and person in such substitutions, e.g.:

John likes classical music and Mary does too (= likes classical music)

John left work early today
Oh? He did yesterday, too (= left work early)

However, EngEng and NAmEng differ in the use of *do* substitution with an auxiliary. In EngEng *do* substitution can occur after most auxiliaries, *do* being inflected for tense (but not person). In NAmEng, *do* cannot be used in such instances. Instead of substitution, a deletion process is used whereby both the verb and its object are deleted. Also, if there are two aspectual auxiliaries, the second (in general) can be deleted. EngEng can also employ this deletion process. The following examples illustrate this:

Context	*Do-substitution* *(EngEng only)*	*Deletion* *(Both NAm and EngEng)*
Did he pass his exams?	*Yes, he did do*	*Yes, he did*
Have you cleaned your room?	*Yes, I have done*	*Yes, I have*
I haven't read this yet	*but I will do*	*but I will*
Will you have finished by next Monday?	*Yes, I will have done*	{*Yes, I will have* {*Yes, I will*
I haven't bought one	*but I may do*	*but I may*
Will he come with us tonight?	*He might do*	*He might*
I haven't thrown them out	*but I should do*	*but I should*
Couldn't you do that later?	*Yes, we could do*	*Yes, we could*
Would you have recognized him?	*No, I wouldn't have done*	{*No, I wouldn't have* {*No, I wouldn't* (informal)

There are certain constructions even within finite verb phrases in which *do*-substitution cannot occur or is unusual in EngEng: when the passive voice is used; when the progressive aspect is used; and when 'semi-auxiliaries' (*happen to*, *be going to*, etc.) are used. (The acceptability of *do*-substitution with progressive aspect, semi-auxiliaries, and negated auxiliaries is also subject to regional variation in EngEng.) Where *do*-substitution is not acceptable, deletion occurs:

	Do-substitution	*Deletion*
Context Passive Voice	*(EngEng only)*	*(NAmEng and EngEng)*
Were you fired?	**Yes, I was done*	*Yes, I was*
Have you been injured?	**Yes, I have been*	{ *Yes, I have been*
	done	{ *Yes, I have*
Progressive Aspect		
Are you working now?	*?Yes, I am doing*	*Yes, I am*
Will you be gardening	*?Yes, we will be*	{ *Yes, we will be*
tomorrow?	*doing*	{ *Yes, we will*
He must have been	*?Yes, he must have*	{ *Yes, he must have been*
driving home	*been doing*	{ *Yes, he must have*
Semi-auxiliary		
I haven't written	*?but I'm going*	*but I'm going to*
to her yet	*to do*	
We didn't mean to	*?We just happened*	*We just happened to*
fall in love	*to do*	
Negated Auxiliary		
I wanted to go	*?but I couldn't do*	*but I couldn't*
Have you read that yet?	*No, I haven't done*	*No, I haven't*
We stayed out late	*but we shouldn't*	*but we shouldn't have*
	have done	

4.1.1.4. Verb phrases

1. Certain verbs, like *give, show, tell, bring* take two objects, a direct object (DO) and an indirect object (IO). The indirect object, which is semantically a 'recipient', can occur with a preposition (usually *to* or *for*) after the DO, or it can occur before the DO without a preposition:

John gave the book to Mary
    DO   IO

John gave Mary the book
    IO   DO

When the DO is a pronoun, USEng requires the order DO + preposition + IO, as does southern EngEng:

USEng and southern EngEng
John gave it to Mary
*John gave Mary it

When both the DO and IO are pronouns, EngEng allows both orderings. It also permits deletion of the preposition in the first pattern, although this construction is somewhat old-fashioned except in northern EngEng:

USEng	*Southern EngEng*	*Northern EngEng*
John gave it to me	*John gave it to me*	*John gave it to me*
	John gave me it	*John gave me it*
		John gave it me

When comparing passive and active versions of a sentence, it can be seen that the DO of the active sentence corresponds to the subject (S) of the passive, and the S of the active corresponds to the object of a *by* prepositional phrase (OP) of the passive (or is deleted):

Active: *John hit Mary*
 S   DO
Passive: *Mary was hit (by John)*
 S   OP

In passive versions of double-object verbs like those above, there are usually two possible nouns which can be subjects—the DO or the IO of the active version:

The book was given to Mary by John
Mary was given the book by John

In USEng, when the active DO is used as the passive subject, the IO must occur with a preposition:

The book was given to Mary by John
*The book was given Mary by John

Both sentences are allowed in EngEng. Also, in some varieties of USEng when the DO is a pronoun, the IO cannot be used as a passive subject:

*Mary was given it by John

Again, however, this is possible in EngEng.

2. The verb *like* may take an infinitive (or infinitive clause) or an *-ing* participle (or clause) as its object:

Infinitive:	*I like to skate*	*I like to photograph animals in the wild*
-ing Participle:	*I like skating*	*I like photographing animals in the wild*

In EngEng the *-ing* participle construction is preferred.

When the object of *like* is a clause and the subject of that clause is not coreferential with the subject of *like*, then a *for ... to* infinitive can be used in USEng. The normal *to* infinitive is usually used in such instances in EngEng.

EngEng and USEng	*USEng*
We'd like you to do this now	*We'd like for you to do this now*

3. In EngEng the copular verbs *seem, act, look* and *sound* can be followed directly by an indefinite noun phrase. In USEng, these verbs must be followed first by the preposition *like; seem* can also be followed by the infinitive *to be*:

EngEng	*USEng/EngEng*
It seemed a long time	*It seemed like a long time*
He seems an intelligent man	*He seems to be an intelligent man*
John acted a real fool	*John acted like a real fool*
That house looks a nice one	*That house looks like a nice one*
That sounds a bad idea	*That sounds like a bad idea*

4. *Come* and *go* may be followed by another verb either in a *to* + infinitive construction or conjoined by *and*:

We are coming to see you soon

$$He\ went\ \left\{ \begin{array}{l} and\ fixed \\ to\ fix \end{array} \right\}\ it\ yesterday$$

When *come* and *go* are uninflected (both for tense and person), *to* and *and* are often dropped in USEng, but not usually in EngEng:

EngEng/NAmEng	*USEng*
We'll come to see you soon	*We'll come see you soon*
Go and fix it now	*Go fix it now*
Can I come and have a cup of coffee with you?	*Can I come have a cup of coffee with you?*

NAmEng is also much more likely than EngEng to delete *to* after *help* when followed by another verb, even when *help* is inflected:

EngEng/NAmEng	*NAmEng*
I'll help to mow the lawn	*I'll help mow the lawn*
John helped us to mow the lawn	*John helped us mow the lawn*

5. When the verb *order* is followed by a passive verb, *to be* is often deleted in USEng, leaving the passive participle:

EngEng/USEng	*USEng*
He ordered the men to be evacuated	*He ordered the men evacuated*
We ordered that to be done immediately	*We ordered that done immediately*

6. The verb *want* can be followed directly by the adverbs *in* and *out* in USEng. In EngEng *want* must be followed first by an infinitive:

EngEng	*USEng*
$I\ wanted\ \left\{ \begin{array}{l} to\ come\ in \\ to\ be\ let\ in \end{array} \right\}$	*I wanted in*
The dog wants to go out	*The dog wants out*

Also, *want* can be used in the sense of 'need' in EngEng with an inanimate subject:

The house wants painting

This is not possible in NAmEng.

7. The verb *wonder* can be followed by a finite clause introduced by *if*, *whether*, or a *wh*-relative pronoun in both varieties:

I wonder if/whether he is coming
I wonder where he went

In EngEng, *wonder* can also be followed by a clause introduced by *that* (*that* is actually optional). In USEng, a periphrastic construction, or a different verb, is used instead:

EngEng   *I wonder (that) he did any work at all!*
USEng   *It's a wonder that he did any work at all!*

EngEng   *I wonder (that) he is not here*
USEng   *I'm surprised that he is not here*

8. The verb *decide* can be used as a causative verb in EngEng:

Non-causative   *He decided to go because of that*
Causative   *That decided him to go* (i.e., 'caused
  him to decide . . .')

In USEng, *decide* cannot be used as a causative; instead, a periphrastic phrase must be used, such as:

Periphrastic causative: *That made him decide to go*

9. There are few verbs in EngEng and USEng which differ in the prepositions or prepositional adverbs they collate with:

EngEng	**USEng**
to battle with/against (the enemy)	*to battle*
to check up on	*to check out*
to fill in (a form)	*to fill out*
to meet (an official = have a meeting)	*to meet with*
to prevent (something becoming . . .)	*to prevent from*
to protest at/against/over (a decision)	*to protest*
to stop (someone doing . . .)	*to stop from*
to talk to	*to talk with/to*
to visit	*to visit with*

10. In EngEng, the negative form of the first person plural imperative, *let's*, can be either *let's not* or, more informally, *don't let's*. Only *let's not* is used in standard USEng.

11. In formal styles, the subjunctive is used more often in USEng than in EngEng in *that*- clauses after verbs of ordering, asking, etc. and in

conditional clauses. Both varieties can replace the subjunctive in such sentences with *that . . . should* + infinitive or with *to* + infinitive, especially in more informal styles:

USEng—formal	*EngEng and USEng—less formal*
We recommended that he be released	*We recommended that he should be released*
It is necessary that you do it	{ *It is necessary that you should do/for you to do it*
We ask that you inform us as soon as possible	*We ask you to inform us as soon as possible*
If this be the case . . .	*If this* { *should be the case, ...* *is the case, ...*

12. Clauses representing hypothetical situations are often introduced by *if*, as in:

   If I had been there, I could have fixed it
   If you (should) need help, please call me
   If this situation were to continue, the authorities would have to take action

   In EngEng, hypothetical clauses can also be formed without using *if* by inverting the subject and verb or first auxiliary:

   Had I been there, I could have fixed it
   Should you need help, please call me
   Were this situation to continue, the authorities would have to take action

   Such constructions are considered very formal in USEng.
13. There is a strong tendency in NAmEng to use simple past tense forms for recently completed events where EngEng would use the present perfect, e.g.:

NAmEng	*So you finally arrived!*
EngEng	*So you've finally arrived!*

   (See also 4.1.3.(6), ScotEng, IrEng.)

4.1.2. The noun phrase

There are few differences between EngEng and USEng as regards the noun phrase, and most are non-systematic in nature.

4.1.2.1. Morphology
1. As with verbal endings (4.1.1.1.(2)), certain noun endings are more productive in USEng than in EngEng, e.g.:

-cian:	*mortician* ('undertaker'); *beautician* ('hairdresser')
-ee:	*retiree, draftee, interviewee*

-ery:	*eatery, bootery, winery, hatchery*
-ster:	*teamster, gamester*

In general, there is a greater tendency in USEng to use nominalizations than in EngEng.

2. For a few words, the derivational ending or the base word that the ending is put on to is different:

EngEng	**USEng**
candidature	*candidacy*
centenary	*centennial*
cookery (book)	*cook (book)*
racialist, racialism (adjective base)	*racist, racism* (noun base)
sparking plug	*spark plug*
stationers	*stationery shop*
transport (no ending)	*transportation*

3. Parallel to nouns being used as verbs (4.1.1.1.(2)), verbs can be used as nouns. Again this tends to occur more in USEng than in EngEng, especially with verb-preposition combinations:

Verb	**Noun**
to cook out (-side)	*a cook-out* ('an outdoor barbeque')
to know how (to do something)	*the know-how*
to run (someone) *around*	*the runaround*
to run down (e.g. a list)	*the rundown*
to be shut in	*a shut-in* ('an invalid')
to stop over (somewhere)	*a stop over*
to try (someone) *out*	*a try-out* ('an audition')

4.1.2.2. Noun class

1. Collective nouns such as *team, faculty, family, government,* etc. often take plural verb agreement and plural pronoun substitution in EngEng but nearly always take singular agreement and singular pronoun substitution in USEng. While both singular and plural agreement and pronoun substitution with collective nouns are found in both varieties, the choice depends on whether the group referred to by the noun is seen as acting as individuals or as a single unit. There is a tendency in EngEng to stress the individuality of the members, which is reflected in plural verb agreement and pronoun substitution, whereas USEng strongly tends to stress the unitary function of the group, which is reflected is singular verb and pronoun forms. Mixed agreement can also be found in USEng:

EngEng   *Your team are doing well this year, aren't they?*

USEng   *Your team is doing well this year* $\begin{cases} \textit{isn't it?} \\ \textit{aren't they?} \end{cases}$

This distinction is particularly striking in the case of sports reports. American newspapers might write of an English football club 'the champion Arsenal and its success' which sounds extremely odd to British people, who would want it to be 'the champions Arsenal and their success'.

2. *Count versus mass nouns.* Count nouns have the following characteristics (among others): they normally occur with an article; that can occur with the indefinite article and cardinal numbers; and they have a plural. Mass nouns, on the other hand, have the opposite characteristics: they can occur with no article; they cannot occur with the indefinite article or cardinal numbers; and they are invariably singular. There are a few nouns which differ in count–mass class membership in the two varieties, e.g.:

(a) *lettuce* has characteristics of both a count and mass noun in EngEng, but it is only a mass noun in many varieties of USEng. It requires a partitive head noun to indicate quantity in USEng:

	EngEng	*USEng* (mass only)
Mass:	*I like lettuce*	*I like lettuce*
Count:	*a lettuce*	*a head of lettuce*
	two lettuces	*two heads of lettuce*

(b) *sport* is a count noun in both varieties but it can also be used as an abstract mass noun in EngEng:

	EngEng	*USEng* (count only)
Count:	*Football is a sport I like*	*Football is a sport I like*
	I like all team sports	*I like all team sports*
Mass:	*John is good at sport*	*John is good at sports*

(c) *accommodation/-s* is an abstract mass noun in both varieties, but instead of being invariably singular as is normal for mass nouns, it is invariably plural in USEng:

EngEng	*USEng*
Good accommodation is hard to find here	*Good accommodations are hard to find here*

3. *Zero plurals.* Some nouns retain the same form for singular and plural (they are said to have a 'zero plural' form), e.g. *sheep*. They differ from invariably singular or plural nouns (like *bread*, *pants*) in that verb agreement does vary from singular to plural even though the noun form does not. There are a few nouns which differ in taking zero plurals in the two varieties, e.g.:

(a) *shrimp* can take a zero plural in USEng but must take a normal plural in EngEng:

EngEng	*USEng*
A shrimp fell on the floor	*A shrimp fell on the floor*
How many shrimps can you eat?	*How many* $\left\{ \begin{array}{l} shrimp \\ shrimps \end{array} \right\}$ *can you eat?*

(b) *Inning* has the plural form *innings* in USEng. In EngEng, the singular form is *innings* and it has a zero plural:

EngEng
There is one innings left to play
There are two innings in a
cricket match

USEng
There is one inning left to play
There are two innings in a
cricket match

(c) When quantitative nouns such as *thousand, million*, etc. are used as modifiers and preceded by a cardinal number, they do not take plural inflection in either variety:

five thousand people
three million dollars

However, when the modified noun is deleted, in EngEng (especially in journalistic EngEng), the plural form of the quantitative noun can be used, while in USEng only the singular can be used:

EngEng only

The government have cut defence spending by three millions

USEng (and EngEng)

The government has cut defense spending by three million

4.1.2.3. Articles

1. There are a number of count nouns in both varieties which do not require an article when used in an abstract-generic sense, usually with certain verbs or prepositions: e.g. *in spring, to go by car, to be at church*. However, there are a few such nouns which have this property in one variety but not the other:

EngEng
to be in hospital

$to \begin{Bmatrix} be\ at \\ go\ to \end{Bmatrix} university$

$to \begin{Bmatrix} be\ in \\ go\ to \end{Bmatrix} a\ class$

USEng
to be in the hospital

$to \begin{Bmatrix} be\ at \\ go\ to \end{Bmatrix} a\ university$

$to \begin{Bmatrix} be\ in \\ go\ to \end{Bmatrix} a\ class$

2. When referring to events in the past, EngEng does not require the definite article before the phrase *next day*. This construction is more usual in written EngEng:

EngEng
Next day, the rains began
I saw him next day

USEng and EngEng
The next day, the rains began
I saw him the next day

3. EngEng does not use the definite article in the phrase *in future* in the meaning 'from now on', while USEng does:

EngEng *In future, I'd like you to pay more attention to detail*
USEng   *In the future, I'd like you to pay more attention . . .*
Both   *In the future, all homes will be heated by solar energy*

4. In temporal phrases beginning with *all*, the definite article can optionally appear before the noun in EngEng: *all afternoon* and *all the afternoon* are equally acceptable. In USEng, the construction without the articles is by far the more frequent. If the sentence in which the phrase appears is negated, both varieties use the construction without the article: *I haven't seen him all year.*

5. In phrases beginning with *half* followed by some unit of measure, EngEng usually requires an indefinite article before the unit of measure. In USEng, the indefinite article can also come before *half*:

EngEng	*USEng*
half an hour	*a half hour* or *half an hour*
half a dozen (eggs)	*a half dozen* or *half a dozen*
half a pound (of carrots)	*a half pound* or *half a pound*

4.1.2.4. Order of attributes

1. In the written standard, especially in newspapers, EngEng generally places personal attributes after the person named, whereas in USEng the attributes tend to precede the name, often without a definite article:

EngEng	*USEng*
John Smith, the lanky Californian teenage tennis star, won another major tournament today	*Lanky Californian teenage tennis star John Smith won another major tournament today*
Margaret Thatcher, the British Prime Minister, arrived in Washington today	*British Prime Minister Margaret Thatcher arrived in Washington today*

2. For names of rivers, EngEng places the word *river* before the name of the river, while NAmEng uses the opposite order:

EngEng	*NAmEng*
the River Thames	*the Mississippi River*
the River Avon	*the Hudson River*

4.1.2.5. Pronouns

1. The indefinite pronoun *one* occurs in EngEng in formal and educated usage, both spoken and written, while in NAmEng it is usually found only in formal written style. *You* is used instead of *one* in informal styles of both varieties:

Formal	*One has to be careful about saying things like that*
Informal	*You have to be careful about saying things like that*

In EngEng when the indefinite pronoun *one* is used in a sentence, any coreferential pronoun in the sentence must also be *one* (or a form of it), while *he* or *she* (or forms of them) can be used in NAmEng:

EngEng and NAmEng (formal/educated)	**NAmEng**
If one tries hard enough, one will always succeed	*If one tries hard enough, he/she will always succeed*
One must be honest with oneself	*One must be honest with himself/herself*
One shouldn't be extravagant with one's money	*One shouldn't be extravagant with his/her money*

2. EngEng uses both reciprocal pronouns *each other* and *one another*, while USEng uses mainly *each other*, with *one another* (like one) being restricted to formal styles.
3. Possessive pronouns have two forms in both varieties: a modifier form and a nominal form:

Modifier   *That is their car*
            This is my cat
Nominal   *That car is theirs*
            This cat is mine

In EngEng, the nominal form can be used as a locative when referring to someone's living quarters, while in USEng the modifier form with noun is used in such cases:

EngEng   *Can we come round to yours tonight?*
            We left his about an hour ago
USEng   *Can we come around to your place tonight?*
            We left his house about an hour ago

4.1.3. Adjectives and adverbs

1. In some varieties of USEng, a comparative adjective can be used in the phrase *all the ADJ* for emphasis or intensification: *Is that all the better you can do? This is all the bigger they grow.* EngEng does not employ this construction; instead, *any* is used with the comparative adjective (as it is also in USEng): *Can't you do any better (than that)? They don't grow any bigger (than this).*
2. The adjective *real* is sometimes used as an adverb in informal USEng as in *a real good meal*. EngEng and more formal USEng can only have the adverbial form *really* in such instances: *a really good meal*.
3. The comparative adjective *different* is usually followed by *from* (or sometimes *to*) in EngEng, while in USEng it is more usually followed by *than*:

EngEng   *This one is different from the last one*
            This is different from what I had imagined
USEng   *This one is different than the last one*
            This is different than what I had imagined

4. One particular adverbial ending is much more productive in USEng than in EngEng: *-wise*. While this ending is used to make nouns into manner adverbials in both varieties, it is also used in USEng to mean 'as far as X is concerned'; as in: *classwise, foodwise, timewise, weatherwise*. This usage is somewhat stigmatized.

5. Adverb placement is somewhat freer in USEng than in EngEng. Those adverbials which can occur medially, before the verb, are placed after the first auxiliary in EngEng if there is one: *They will* never *agree to it. You could* always *have called us first*. In USEng, such adverbs can occur either before or after the auxiliary: *They* never *will agree to it*, or *They will* never *agree to it. You* probably *could have done it yourself*, or *You could* probably *have done it yourself*.

6. The adverbs *yet* and *still* cannot occur with the simple past tense in EngEng, but they can do so in USEng. EngEng uses the present perfect in such cases.

EngEng and USEng (present perfect)	**USEng only (simple past)**
I haven't bought one yet	*I didn't buy one yet*
Have you read it already?	*Did you read it already?*

7. When the verb *to be* is used in the perfective with the meaning 'to go' or 'to come', the pronominal place adverbs *here* and *there* can be deleted in EngEng and CanEng, but not in USEng:

EngEng and CanEng	*Has the milkman been yet?*
	Did you go to the market with them yesterday?
	No, I'd already been
USEng	*Has the milkman been here yet?*
	Did you go to the market with them yesterday?
	No, I'd already been there

8. The ordinals *first(ly)*, *second(ly)*, etc. are used in both varieties as conjunctive adverbs in the listing of objects, actions, ideas, etc. While both varieties also use the enumerative adverbial phrase *first of all*, only USEng regularly uses *second of all*, *third of all*, etc. in such passages, although this would not be found in formal writing.

9. The adverb *momentarily* means 'for a moment' in both varieties. However, in USEng it can also mean 'in a moment':

Both	*He was momentarily stunned*	(for a moment)
USEng only	*I'll do it momentarily*	(in a moment)

Similarly, the adverb *presently* means 'soon' in both varieties, but in USEng can also mean 'at present' (when the verb is in the present tense):

Both	*They will be here presently*	(soon)
USEng only	*They are presently here*	(at present)

10. Adverbs ending in *-ward* in EngEng denote a purely directional motion while those ending in *-wards* can denote manner of movement

also: *backward* ('movement to the back'), *backwards* ('movement back-first'). In USEng -*ward* no longer has a purely directional denotation for most speakers and such adverbs are used interchangeably, e.g.: *front-ward(s)*. NAmEng has the forms *toward* and *towards* (identical in meaning). EngEng has only *towards*.

11. The time adverb *anymore* is used in both varieties in negative contexts, as in *I don't do that anymore* (= 'I no longer do that?'). In some dialects of NAmEng (particularly Pennsylvania, upstate New York, Ontario and the Mid-West), *anymore* can also be used in positive contexts with the meaning 'nowadays'. Implied in this usage is that whatever is being said to happen nowadays did not use to be the case: the sentence *He comes here a lot anymore* means that he comes here a lot nowadays and did not use to come here a lot. (For a possible origin of this feature, see 5.2.2.)

12. *Ever* can be used as an intensifier (without meaning 'at some time') in both varieties, but in different contexts. In EngEng it is commonly used with the intensifier *so* before adjectives:

EngEng   *She is ever so nice*
        That match was ever so close

In NAmEng, *ever* can be used informally to intensify verbs in exclamations which have subject-verb inversion:

NAmEng   *Did he ever hit the ball hard!*
        Has she ever grown!
        Am I ever tired!

13. In CanEng, the adverbial phrase *as well* can occur sentence initially, whereas in EngEng and USEng it usually appears after the item it modifies:

CanEng   *This has always applied to men. As well, it*
                now applies to women
EngEng and USEng   *This has always applied to men. It now*
                applies to women as well

14. NAmEng has two usages of *over* which are much less common elsewhere. First, *over* can mean 'again', in the sense of repeating an action, usually in connection with the verb *do*:

This is no good—I'll have to do it over
(cf. EngEng: (*all over*) *again*)

Second, it has a locative usage, meaning 'to my place':

We're having a party—why don't you come over?

EngEng more commonly uses *round* in this sense.

4.1.4. Prepositions

1. There are a few prepositions which differ in form in the two varieties:

   EngEng   USEng

   behind   in back of   as in *I put it* $\left\{\begin{array}{l} behind \\ in\ back\ of \end{array}\right\}$ *the shed*

   out of   out   as in *He threw it* $\left\{\begin{array}{l} out\ of \\ out \end{array}\right\}$ *the window*

   round   around   as in *She lives just* $\left\{\begin{array}{l} round \\ around \end{array}\right\}$ *the corner*

2. Some prepositions which are used identically in most contexts in both EngEng and USEng differ in usage in certain contexts. The majority of such cases occur in expressions of time.
(a) Difference in preposition used:
(i) In phrases indicating duration of time, EngEng uses *for* where NAmEng has a choice of *for* or *in*:

	EngEng and NAmEng	**NAmEng only**
I haven't seen him:	*for weeks*	*in weeks*
for ages	*in ages*	

(ii) EngEng speakers use the preposition *at*, meaning 'time when', with holiday seasons, as in *at the weekend, at Christmas* (the season, not the day). USEng speakers generally use *over* in such cases: *over the weekend, over Christmas*. EngEng also permits *over* in these cases, and NAmEng also has *on the weekend*.
(iii) In USEng the preposition *through* can mean 'up to and including', as in *Monday through Friday, September 1 through October 15*. In EngEng the 'inclusiveness' must be stated separately if ambiguity is possible: e.g. *Monday to Friday (inclusive)* or *Monday up to and including Friday*.
(iv) In expressing clock-time, EngEng uses the prepositions *to* and *past* the hour while USEng also can use *of, till* and *after* (this differs regionally in the USA):

EngEng and USEng	**USEng only**
twenty to three	*twenty of three or twenty till three*
five past eight	*five after eight*

(v) *In* and *on* have some differences in non-temporal contexts:

EngEng	**USEng**
to be in a team	*to be on a team*
to live in a street	*to live on a street*
to be in a sale	*to be on sale*
	(Note: *on sale* in EngEng simply means *for sale*.)

(b)   Difference in presence of a preposition:
(i)   The preposition (usually *on*) is often omitted in USEng before a specific date or day of the week that indicates a time removed from the present:

EngEng	**USEng**
The sale started on Jan. 1st	*The sale started Jan. 1*
(said: 'on January the first')	(said: 'January first')
I'll do it on Sunday	*I'll do it Sunday*

(ii) The preposition can be deleted in USEng before temporal nouns indicating repetition or habitual action (the nouns must become plural if deletion occurs):

EngEng and USEng	**USEng**
He works by day and studies at night	*He works days and studies nights*
On Saturdays we go to London	*Saturdays we go to London*

(iii) In EngEng temporal prepositional phrases, inversion of the noun and the words *this*, *that*, *next* or *last* can occur in formal styles: *on Sunday next*, *during January last*. Such inversion does not occur in USEng, and the preposition is deleted in the uninverted forms (as in (i) above): *next Sunday*, *last January*.
(iv) In phrases denoting a period of time from or after a given time, the preposition *from* is often deleted in EngEng, but cannot be deleted in USEng:

EngEng	**USEng**
a week this Tuesday	*a week from this Tuesday*

EngEng also allows inversion in such phrases with no preposition: *Saturday fortnight, Tuesday week*. This does not occur in USEng.

(v)   In EngEng, there is a difference in meaning between the phrases *to be home* and *to be at home*:

Is John at home?	(Is he physically there?)
Is John home?	(Has he returned there?)

USEng can use the second phrase (without the preposition) in the meaning of the first.

(vi) In EngEng, the preposition *from* can be deleted after the verbs *excused* and *dismissed*:

He was excused games at school
He was dismissed the service

This is not possible in USEng.

3.   In interrogative structures involving *how* + certain adjectives, many varieties of USEng employ the preposition *of*:

How big of a house is it?
I wondered how small of a piece you wanted

Such structures are not possible in EngEng.

4. In sentences such as *The cake has flowers on it, The box with toys in it is mine,* where an inanimate concrete object is designated as having (or not having) a concrete object *in, on, round* or *off* it, the coreferential pronoun *it* can be deleted from the prepositional phrase in EngEng, but not in USEng:

EngEng   *USEng*
The soup has carrots in   The soup has carrots in it
I want some paper with lines on   I want some paper with lines on it
This shirt has two buttons off   This shirt has two buttons off it
What kind is that tree with   What kind is that tree with
flowers round?   flowers around it?
I'd like toast without butter on   I'd like toast without butter on it.

4.1.5. Subordinators

1. The complex subordinators *as . . . as* and *so . . . as* are used with different frequencies in the two varieties. *So . . . as* is fairly infrequent in USEng, being used mainly at the beginning of a clause, while in EngEng it tends to be used more than *as . . . as*:

EngEng   *USEng*
It's not so far as I thought it was   It's not as far as I thought it was
So long as you're happy, we'll stay   As long as you're happy, we'll stay
Now we don't go there so much   Now we don't go there as much
 (as we used to)   (as we used to)
That one isn't so nice (as the other)   That one isn't as nice (as the other)

In cases where *as . . . as* is preferred in EngEng and used at the beginning of a clause, the first *as* may be dropped:

EngEng   *USEng*
Strange as it may seem, . . .   As strange as it may seem, . . .
Much as I would like to go, . . .   As much as I would like to go, . . .

2. In EngEng, the adverbs *immediately* and *directly* can function as subordinators. In USEng, they must modify a subordinator, such as *after*:

EngEng   *USEng*
Immediately we went, it began   Immediately after we went, it
 to rain   began to rain
Go to his office directly you arrive   Go to his office directly after
                                           you arrive

3. For many, particularly older, USEng speakers, *why* can function as a subordinator, especially in conditional sentences:

    If you have any problems, why, just ask for help

4.2. Spelling and punctuation differences

4.2.1. Standard spellings

There are sets of regular spelling differences that exist between the English and American varieties of English. Some are due to American innovations or to overt attempts at spelling regularization (especially by Noah Webster in his 1806 dictionary). Others simply reflect the fact that English spelling was variable in earlier times and the two varieties chose different variants as their standard. Below is a list exemplifying the major spelling differences. No attempt has been made to include every word falling under the particular spelling correspondence; we have indicated if the set is a restricted one. CanEng usage in some cases follows USEng, in others EngEng, and in yet others is variable.

1. **EngEng: -our**   **USEng: -or**   (but not in words ending
   colour   *color*   in *-or* signifying persons,
   favour   *favor*   e.g. *emperor, governor* in
   honour   *honor*   both varieties; these
   labour   *labor*   spellings are also widely
   odour   *odor*   used in AusEng, especially
   vapour   *vapor*   in Victoria)

2. **EngEng: -ou-**   **USEng: -o-**   (restricted lexical set;
   mould   *mold*   cf. *boulder* in both varieties)
   moult   *molt*
   smoulder   *smolder*

3. **EngEng: -ae/oe-**   **USEng: -e-**   (in Greek borrowings;
   anaesthetic   *anesthetic*   USEng sometimes uses
   encyclopaedia   *encyclopedia*   EngEng spelling in
   mediaeval   *medieval*   scholarly works)
   amoeba   *ameba*
   foetus   *fetus*
   manoeuvre   *maneuver*

4. **EngEng: en-**   **USEng: in-**   (restricted; cf. *envelope*,
   encase   *incase*   *incur* in both varieties;
   enclose   *inclose*   *inquire* also used in
   endorse   *indorse*   EngEng; EngEng spelling
   enquire   *inquire*   preferred in USEng in all
   ensure   *insure*   but last three items)
   enure   *inure*

5. **EngEng: -dgement**   **USEng: -dgment**   (EngEng spelling also
   abridgement   *abridgment*   possible in USEng)
   acknowledgement   *acknowledgment*
   judgement   *judgment*

6. **EngEng: -re**   **USEng: -er**
   centre   *center*
   fibre   *fiber*
   litre   *liter*
   metre   *meter*
   spectre   *specter*
   theatre   *theater*

7. **EngEng: -ce**   **USEng: -se**
   defence   *defense*
   licence (n.)   *license* (n. and v.)
   offence   *offense*
   practice (n.)   *practise* or *practice* (n.)
   pretence   *pretense*

8. **EngEng: -ise**   **USEng: -ize**   (USEng spelling is also
   apologise   *apologize*   possible in EngEng;
   capitalise   *capitalize*   CanEng spelling usually has
   dramatise   *dramatize*   -ize when the stem is
   glamorise   *glamorize*   transparent—*capitalize,*
   naturalise   *naturalize*   *glamorize, naturalize*—and
   satirise   *satirize*   -ise when it is not—
                                                    apologise, realise; EngEng
                                                    and NAmEng both
                                                    normally have *advertise*)

9. **EngEng: -xion**   **USEng: -ction**   (USEng spelling also
   connexion   *connection*   possible in EngEng;
   deflexion   *deflection*   restricted, cf. *inspection*
   inflexion   *inflection*   and *complexion* in both
   retroflexion   *retroflection*   varieties)

10. **EngEng: doubled**   **USEng: single**   (only before an ending that
    consonant   **consonant**   starts with a vowel, stress
    counsellor   *counselor*   not on last syllable of stem;
    kidnapper   *kidnaper*   EngEng spelling also used
    levelled   *leveled*   in USEng)
    libellous   *libelous*
    quarrelling   *quarreling*
    travelled   *traveled*
    worshipping   *worshiping*

11. **EngEng:**   **USEng:**   (before an ending that
    single -l-   **double -l-**   starts with a consonant or
    fulfilment   *fulfillment*   at the end of a polysyllabic
    instalment   *installment*   word that has stress on the
    skilful   *skillful*   last syllable)

enthral	*enthrall*
instil	*instill*
fulfil	*fulfill*

12. **EngEng: -gg-**   **USEng: -g-**   (restricted to a few words)

faggot ('bundle of sticks')	*fagot* (but *faggot* slang, 'homosexual')
waggon	*wagon*

13. **EngEng: -st**   **USEng: no ending**   (restricted to a few words; USEng spelling also possible in EngEng; spelling differences reflected in pronunciation)

amidst	*amid*
amongst	*among*
whilst	*while*

14. **Miscellaneous**

EngEng	**USEng**	
buses	*busses* or *buses*	
cheque (banking)	*check*	
draught	*draft*	
gaol	*jail*	
gauge	*gage* or *gauge*	
jewellery	*jewelry*	
kerb	*curb*	
moustache	*mustache*	
plough	*plow*	
programme	*program*	
pyjamas	*pajamas* or *pyjamas*	
sorbet	*sherbet*	(different pronunciation)
speciality	*specialty*	(different pronunciation)
storey (of a building)	*story*	
sulphur	*sulfur*	
toffee	*taffy*	(different pronunciation)
tsar	*czar*	
tyre	*tire*	
whisky	*whiskey*	
woollen	*woolen*	

15. **EngEng: hyphenated words**   **USEng: fused or two separate words**   (in compounds and words with stressed prefixes; hyphen is usually kept in USEng if identical vowels are brought together or if stem begins with capital

ash-tray	*ashtray* (also EngEng)
book-keeper	*bookkeeper*

day-dream	daydream	letter, e.g. *anti-British,*
dry-dock	dry dock	*pre-eminent*)
flower-pot	flower pot	
note-paper	note paper	
anti-aircraft	antiaircraft	
co-operate	cooperate	
neo-classical	neoclassical	
pre-ignition	preignition	
pseudo-intellectual	pseudointellectual	
ultra-modern	ultramodern	

16. **EngEng: retains**   **USEng: diacritics**
    French diacritics   **not necessary**

café	cafe
élite	elite
entrée	entree
fête	fete
fiancée	fiancee
matinée	matinee

4.2.2. 'Sensational' spellings

In the USA, and increasingly in Britain, many sensational (and non-standard) spellings which usually involve simplification of the spelling to reflect more closely the pronunciation are used to attract attention, especially in advertising and in tabloid newspapers; they may also be used on roadsigns to save space. The list below gives a sample of common nouns often spelled in a nonstandard way; a list of proper nouns (brand names especially) would be exceedingly long.

Sensational	*Standard*
bi	buy
donut	doughnut
hi	high
kool	cool
kwik	quick
lo	low
nite, tonite	night, tonight
pleez	please
rite	right
sox	socks
thanx	thanks
tho	though
thru, thruway	through, throughway
U	you
Xing	crossing

4.2.3. Punctuation

There are very few punctuation differences between 'American' and 'English' types of English, and printers and publishers vary in their preference even within the two areas. Typically, however, British usage favours having a lower case letter for the first word of a sentence following a colon, as in:

There is only one problem: the government does not spend sufficient money on education

whereas American usage more often favours a capital letter:

There is only one problem: The government does not spend sufficient money on education

Also, normal British usage is to have a full-stop after a closing quotation mark, as in:

We are often told that 'there is not enough money to go round'.

while American usage has the full-stop (AmEng *period*) before the closing quotation marks:

We are often told that 'there is not enough money to go round.'

Note, however, that if a whole sentence is devoted to a quotation, usage agrees in having the full-stop before the quotation marks:

'There is not enough money to go round.'

4.3. Vocabulary differences

Perhaps the most noticeable differences between EngEng and NAmEng involve vocabulary. There are thousands of words which either differ in total meaning, or in one particular sense or usage, or are totally unknown in the other variety. (There are also a large number of idioms and colloquialisms which differ in the two varieties, but these will not be discussed here.)

Vocabulary differences between the two varieties are due to several factors. The most obvious is that new objects and experiences were encountered in North America which needed naming, either by adapting EngEng vocabulary or by creating new words: e.g. *corn* is the general English term for grain and denotes the most common grain crop, which is wheat in England but maize in North America; the word *robin* denotes a small, red-breasted warbler in England but a large, red-breasted thrush in North America; the words *panhandle* (the narrow part of a state extending outward like a pan's handle) and *butte* (an abrupt isolated hill with a flat top) denote features not found in Britain.

Technological and cultural developments which have occurred since the divergence of two varieties have also been a cause of differences in vocabulary, e.g. terms for parts of cars: US *windshield*, Eng *windscreen*; US *trunk*, Eng *boot*; terminology from different sports: US (from baseball) *home run, bunt, pitcher*; Eng (from cricket) *pitch, wicket, bowler*, etc.; differences in institutions of education: US *high school* (14–18 year olds), *major* (= *main subject*), *co-ed* (female student); Eng *public school* (= *private school*), *form* (educational level), *reader* (= *associate professor*), etc.

A third reason for vocabulary differences is the influence of other languages. USEng has borrowed many words (some of which have found their way into EngEng) from a variety of languages, including: American Indian languages—*hickory* (type of tree related to walnut), *hooch* (alcoholic liquor), *moccasin, muskie* (type of freshwater fish), *squash, toboggan*, and many words for indigenous flora, fauna and geographical features; Spanish— *mesa* (plateau), *tornado* (whirlwind), *tortilla* (thin flat maize bread); African languages—*goober* (peanut), *jazz, banjo*; and Yiddish—*schmaltz* (excessive sentimentality), *schlep* (to drag, carry), *schlock* (rubbish).

Finally, independent linguistic change within each variety may be the cause of some differences. One variety may preserve archaisms which the other has lost, or may introduce new meanings for old words which the other has not introduced. CanEng examples of archaisms include *chesterfield* (sofa, couch) and *reeve* (mayor, chief local government officer).

We can divide vocabulary differences into four main categories, although there is some overlap.

1. *Same word, different meaning.* This is the category of words which is potentially the most problematic for both foreign and native speakers of one variety, but such examples are few in number. They include:

Word	**EngEng meaning**	**USEng meaning**
homely	'down to earth, domestic' (= *US homey*)	'ugly (of people)'
nervy	'nervous'	'bold, full of nerve, cheeky'
pants	'underpants'	'trousers'
pavement	'footpath, sidewalk'	'road surface'
to tick off	'to scold'	'to make angry'

2. *Same word, additional meaning in one variety.* There are quite a few words of this type, some of which can cause communication problems between speakers of the two varieties. Often the additional meaning is due to a metaphorical extension of the common meaning:

   Additional meaning in USEng

Word	**Meaning in common**	**Additional meaning in USEng**
bathroom	'room with bath or shower and sink'	'room with toilet only'

cute	'endearing' (e.g. of kittens)	'attractive, charming' (e.g. of adult people)
dumb	'mute'	'stupid'
good	'fine, nice', etc.	'valid' (as of tickets, special offers)
regular	'consistent, habitual'	'average' (as in size), 'normal'
school	'institution of education at elementary level'	'all institutions of education, including universities'
to ship	'to transport by ship'	'to transport by ship, train, plane or truck'

Additional meaning in EngEng

Word	Meaning in common	Additional meaning in EngEng
frontier	'a wild, open space'	'border between two countries'
leader	'one who commands, guides, directs, is in front'	'an editorial'
to mind	'to heed, obey'	'to look after' (as in *mind your head, mind the children*)
rug	'a thick (usually wool) carpet'	'a thick (usually wool) wrap or coverlet' (USEng *afghan*)
smart	'intelligent'	'well-groomed'
surgery	'a medical operation or operating room'	'an office of any doctor'

3. *Same word, difference in style, connotation, frequency of use.* While words differing in style, connotation, or frequency will usually be understood by speakers of the other variety, it is the use of these types of words which often reveals which variety of English a person has learned. The example words below are marked for differences in style (formal versus informal), connotation (positive versus negative) or frequency (common versus uncommon):

Word	EngEng usage	USEng usage
autumn	common; all styles	uncommon; poetic or formal (*fall* used instead)
clever ('smart, dexterous')	common; positive	less common; usually negative (i.e. 'sly')
to fancy ('to like, want')	common; informal	uncommon
fortnight	common; all styles	uncommon (archaic); poetic
perhaps	all styles	somewhat formal (*maybe* used instead)
quite (as in *quite good*)	negative or neutral	positive
row (/raʊ/; 'quarrel, disturbance')	common	uncommon

4. *Same concept or item, different word.* The majority of lexical differences between the two varieties are of this type. There are two sub-types within this category: that in which the corresponding word is not widely known in the other variety, and that in which the corresponding word is known. Examples of the first type include:

USEng only	*Corresponds to EngEng*
emcee	*compère*
faucet	*tap*
muffler (on car)	*silencer*
rookie	*first year member* (e.g. on a team)
sophomore	*second year student*
washcloth	*face flannel*

EngEng only	*Corresponds to USEng*
dynamo	*generator*
hire purchase	*installment buying*
nought	*zero*
queue	*line*
spanner	*monkey wrench*
treacle	*molasses*

Examples of the second type include:

USEng	*EngEng*
to call (by telephone)	*to ring*
can	*tin*
to check ('to make a check mark')	*to tick*
couch, davenport	*sofa*
game (sports)	*match*
gas	*petrol*
to make a reservation	*to book*
sidewalk	*(paved streetside) path*

Finally, by way of further illustration, we give a brief and arbitrary selection of words that differ in particular semantic spheres. Note that some words, while identical in one semantic sphere or part of speech, can be different in another: e.g. both varieties use the words *hood* and *bonnet* to refer to two distinct types of head covering, but when referring to the covering of a car engine, USEng uses *hood* and EngEng uses *bonnet*. Likewise, while both varieties have the verb to *flex* with identical meaning, the noun *a flex* is used only in EngEng (and is unknown in USEng) to refer to an electric cord.

Food and cooking

USEng	*EngEng*
cookie (plain)	*biscuit* (sweet)
biscuit	*scone*
cracker	*biscuit* (savoury)
dessert	*pudding*

pudding	custard
custard	egg custard
jello	jelly
jelly	jam
crepe	pancake
hamburger meat	mince
roast (noun)	joint
eggplant	aubergine
zucchini	courgette
to broil	to grill
stove	cooker
bowl (e.g. for pudding)	basin
pitcher	jug

Clothing and accessories

USEng	EngEng
garter	suspender
suspenders	braces
underpants (women's)	knickers
knickers	knickerbockers
smock	overall
overalls	dungarees
sweater (pullover)	jumper
jumper	dress worn over blouse
undershirt	vest
vest	waistcoat
pantyhose	tights
tuxedo	dinner jacket
barrette	hairslide
changepurse	purse
purse	handbag
diaper	nappy

Household

USEng	EngEng
living room	sitting room
yard	garden
garden	vegetable or flower garden
buffet	sideboard
flashlight	torch
floorlamp	standard lamp
garbage can	dustbin
outlet/socket	power point
sheers	net curtains

Commerce

USEng	EngEng
mortician	undertaker

realtor	*estate agent*
traveling salesman	*commercial traveller*
drug store/pharmacy	*chemist's shop*
hardware store	*ironmongers*
liquor store	*off-licence store*
trade (noun)	*custom*

Transportation

USEng	EngEng
baby buggy	*pram (perambulator)*
station wagon	*estate car*
trailer/camper/mobile home	*caravan*
pullman car (railway)	*sleeping car*
flatcar (railway)	*truck*
truck	*lorry*
pedestrain underpass	*subway*
subway	*underground railway*

4.3.1. Lexical Americanization

Ever since the advent of the electronic media, starting with the importation of American films with soundtracks into Britain and other English-speaking countries from 1928 onwards, originally NAmEng words have been finding their way into other forms of English, quite often replacing indigenous words.

Words which came into EngEng from NAmEng in the years before and after the Second World War include:

(car) battery	formerly	*accumulator*
briefcase		*portfolio*
raincoat		*mackintosh*
radio		*wireless*
sweater		*jumper*
dessert		*sweet*
peanut		*monkeynut*
soft drinks		*minerals*

A few words have crossed the Atlantic in the opposite direction—*penny*, *smog* and *copper* 'policeman' are often cited as examples. But because of the dominance of the USA in the media, most of the traffic has been from NAmEng into other varieties.

It is interesting to see that this process continues, and that this book itself provides clear evidence for this. Since our first edition was published over 25 years ago, a number of the features we originally described as being typical only of NAmEng are no longer so. Of the words we have listed in 4.3, British people can now in fact be heard using *cute* to mean 'attractive'. And retailers in Britain now sell *cookies*, *cans* of drink, *crepes*, and *regular* servings of coffee, even if ordinary people do not use these words so much. The word *rookie* can be found in the sports pages of news-papers, where players are just as likely now to be *on* a team rather than *in* it. And if younger people say they are going to *call*, they are more likely to mean telephone rather than visit. The word *billion* has almost entirely lost its original British meaning of 'a million million' and now mostly means 'a thousand million', though one can never be quite sure. And a large number of British people now say *truck* rather than *lorry*, while the word *washcloth* is now very common. Young men now sometimes wear a *tuxedo*. And *smart* and *dumb* are now sometimes understood to mean *clever* and *stupid*.

And while British people have always pronounced *November 1st* as 'November the first', they can now also be heard saying 'November first' in the NAmEng way, and, sometimes, *2008* as 'two thousand eight' rather than the typical British 'two thousand and eight'.

|5|

Scottish and Irish English

5.1. Scottish English

English has been spoken in the south-east of Scotland for as long as it has been spoken in England. In the south-west of Scotland it dates from the Middle Ages. And in the Highlands and Islands of northern and western Scotland, English has been spoken for only 200 years or so, and indeed Gaelic is still the native language of several tens of thousands of speakers from these areas.

A standardized language based on southern Scottish varieties and known as Scots was used at the Scottish court and in literature until the Reformation. Since that time, however, Scots has at least partly lost its status as a separate language and has gradually been replaced in most educated usage by Standard English. The result is that today educated Scottish people speak and write a form of Standard English which is grammatically and lexically not very different from that used elsewhere, although they speak it with a very obviously Scottish accent. In the Highlands, where English was initially learned only in school, forms relatively close to Scottish Standard English are used by all speakers.

5.1.1. ScotEng pronunciation: vowels

ScotEng pronunciation is very different from that of most other varieties and may be difficult to understand for students who have learned EngEng or NAmEng. Table 5.1 and the recording illustrate a typical ScotEng vowel system.

It will be observed at once that there are fewer vowels in this system than in any of the other varieties we have examined. This is due to the following factors:

1. ScotEng is rhotic. Therefore, the RP vowels /ɪə/, /ɛə/, /ʊə/ and /ɜː/, which arose in RP as a result of the loss of non-prevocalic /r/, do not

Table 5.1. ScotEng vowels*

/i/	*bee, peer*
/e/	*bay, pair*
/ɛ/	*bed, merry, fern*
/ɪ/	*bid, bird, butter, wanted*
/ʌ/	*putt, hurry, fur, sofa*
/a/	*bad, marry, bard, path, father, calm*
/u/	*put, boot, poor*
/o/	*boat*
/ɔ/	*pot, long, cough, fork, paw*
/ai/	*buy*
/au/	*bout*
/ɔi/	*boy*

*The words in Table 5.1. are also used in the recording for NIrEng (see page 103).

occur in ScotEng, and words such as *sawed* and *soared* are distinct. Furthermore, it is a particular characteristic of ScotEng that even short vowels remain distinct before /r/. As a consequence of this, the following pairs are distinguished only by the presence or absence of /r/:

bee	/bi/	*beer*	/bir/
bay	/be/	*bear*	/ber/
fen	/fɛn/	*fern*	/fɛrn/
bid	/bɪd/	*bird*	/bɪrd/
hut	/hʌt/	*hurt*	/hʌrt/
bad	/bad/	*bard*	/bard/
moo	/mu/	*moor*	/mur/
row	/ro/	*roar*	/ror/
pock	/pɔk/	*pork*	/pɔrk/

Note that *fern, bird, hurt* all have *different* vowels; however, they are often merged in middle-class speech.

2. The RP distinction between /æ/ and /ɑ:/ does not exist in most ScotEng varieties. We write /a/ for the vowel of *bad, bard, calm*, etc. Note that *Pam* and *palm* are therefore homonyms—/pam/. However, some middle-class speakers do have this distinction, probably as a result of the influence of RP.

3. The RP distinction between /ʊ/ and /u:/ does not exist in most types of ScotEng. *Pool* and *pull* are homonyms—/pul/.

4. There is no RP-type distinction between /ɒ/ and /ɔ:/. We write /ɔ/ for both *cot* and *caught*.

5. Phonetically, the ScotEng vowels are monophthongs (with the exceptions of /ai/ = [ɛɪ]~[ɐɪ]; /au/ = [ɜʉ]; and /ɔi/). Both /ɪ/ = [ɪ⊢ ~ə] and /ʌ/ are central vowels, and /u/ = [ʉ].

6. All vowels in ScotEng are of approximately the same length, so that /ɛ/ often sounds longer than in EngEng, while /i/ sounds shorter than

EngEng /iː/. However, there is a complication in that all the vowels of ScotEng, except /ɪ/ and /ʌ/, are subject to the *Scottish Vowel Length Rule*. This rule has the effect that vowels are longer before /v/, /ð/, /z/, /r/ and word-finally than they are elsewhere. Thus the /i/ in *leave* is longer than the /i/ in *lead*, and the /e/ in *pair* is longer than the /e/ in *pale*. Word-final vowels remain long even if a suffix is added. There is thus a distinction of length in ScotEng between the vowels of pairs such as the following:

Short	**Long**
greed	*agreed*
wade	*weighed*
fraud	*flawed*
toad	*towed*
mood	*mooed*
tide	*tied*
loud	*allowed*

7. In words such as *serenity, obscenity*, the second syllable is often pronounced with /i/, as it is in *serene, obscene*, rather than with /ɛ/ as in RP.

5.1.2. ScotEng pronunciation: consonants

1. ScotEng consistently and naturally preserves a distinction between /ʍ/ and /w/: *which* /ʍɪtʃ/, *witch* /wɪtʃ/.
2. Initial /p/, /t/, /k/ are often unaspirated in ScotEng.
3. The consonant /r/ is most usually a flap [ɾ], as in *fern* [fɛɾn] (cf. RP [fɜːn], USEng [fəɹn]). Some middle-class speakers, however, use the frictionless continuant [ɹ]. These are usually the same speakers who have merged /ɪ/, /ɜ/, /ʌ/ before /r/ (see above); thus they have *fern* as [fəɹn].
4. The glottal stop [ʔ] is a frequent realization of non-initial /t/.
5. /l/ may be dark in all positions; e.g. *lilt* [ɫəɫt].
6. The velar fricative /x/ occurs in a number of specifically ScotEng words, e.g. *loch* [lɔx] 'lake'; *dreich* [drix] 'dull'. In Scots dialects /x/ occurs in many other words, e.g. *nicht* [nəxt] = *night* (ScotEng [nɛɪt]).

5.1.3. Non-systematic differences between ScotEng and EngEng pronunciation

A few words have distinctively Scottish, or at least non-RP, pronunciations in Scotland:

	ScotEng	*RP*
length	/lɛnθ/	/lɛŋθ/
raspberry	/rasbɛrɪ/	/rɑːzbrɪ/
realize	/riʌláiz/	/ríəlaiz/
though	/θo/	/ðou/
tortoise	/tɔrtɔiz/	/tɔːtəs/
with	/wɪθ/	/wɪð/

5.1.4. ScotEng grammar

Most of the grammatical differences between ScotEng and EngEng are found at the level of informal speech. They include the following:

1. In many forms of ScotEng main verb *have* does not require *do*-support, even with dynamic meanings (see 4.1.1.2.) and it can also occur in and with phonologically reduced forms:

    Had you a good time?
    Yes, we had.
    Have you coffee with breakfast?
    Yes, I have.
    We'd a good time.
    I've coffee with breakfast.
    We HAD a good time.
    I HAVE coffee with breakfast.
    We hadn't a good time.
    I haven't coffee with breakfast.

    That is, main verb and auxiliary *have* behave alike; and stative *have* also behaves like dynamic *have*. This is also true of many forms of IrEng.

2. As in NAmEng, *will* has replaced *shall* in most contexts. ScotEng goes further than NAmEng in having *will* with first person subjects in questions:

    ScotEng   *Will I put out the light?*
    Others   *Shall/Should I put out the light?*

3. There is a tendency not to contract the negative element *not* in ScotEng, especially in yes–no questions. If an auxiliary is present in a negated sentence, the auxiliary usually contracts.

ScotEng	**EngEng**
Is he not going?	*Isn't he going?*
Did you not see it?	*Didn't you see it?*
He'll not go	*He won't go*
You've not seen it	*You haven't seen it*

4. In sentences like the following, *need* is a full verb with a verbal complement, as in USEng, rather than a modal, as in EngEng (see 4.1.1.2.(1g)):

    ScotEng   *I don't need to do that*
    EngEng   *I needn't do that*

    Need can occur with a passive participle as its object, as it can in some regional US dialects, whereas most other varieties of English require the passive infinitive or present participle:

    ScotEng   *My hair needs washed*
    EngEng   *My hair needs washing*
              My hair needs to be washed

5. *Want* and *need* can have a directional adverb as object as in USEng (see 4.1.1.4.(6)):

   He wants/needs out

6. Certain stative verbs, especially *want* and *need*, can be used in the progressive aspect in ScotEng:

   I'm needing a cup of tea

7. As in USEng, *yes* can occur in ScotEng with non-perfective forms of the verb, while in EngEng it can only occur with the perfective (see 4.1.3.(6)):

   ScotEng   *Did you buy one yet?*
   EngEng   *Have you bought one yet?*

   ScotEng   *He is here yet*
   EngEng   *He is still here*

8. In EngEng the adverbial particle in compound verbs tends to come after the direct object, while in ScotEng it remains directly after the verb, as in many varieties of NAmEng:

ScotEng	**EngEng**
He turned out the light	*He turned the light out*
They took off their coats	*They took their coats off*

   All of the above grammatical features are also found in NIrEng.

5.1.5. ScotEng vocabulary and idioms

The vocabulary of Scots and nonstandard Scottish dialects differs very considerably from that of Standard English, to the extent that dictionaries or glossaries may be necessary for reading literature in Scots (e.g. Burns, McDiarmid). ScotEng, on the other hand, differs much less in its vocabulary from other varieties of English. The differences, nevertheless, are numerous enough. We give a brief list and discussion here of a few of the ScotEng lexical items which may be encountered.

	ScotEng	**EngEng**
1.	*ashet*	*serving dish*
2.	*aye*	*yes*
3.	*brae*	*incline, hill*
4.	*bramble*	*blackberry*
5.	*burn*	*stream*
6.	*carry-out*	*take-away*
7.	*dram*	*drink*
8.	*dreich*	*dull*
9.	*folk*	*people*
10.	*haar*	*sea mist*
11.	*infirmary*	*hospital*
12.	*to jag*	*to prick, jab*

13. *janitor*   *caretaker*
14. *loch*   *lake*
15. *to mind*   *to remember*
16. *outwith*   *outside*
17. *pinkie*   *little finger*
18. *provost*   *mayor*
19. *rone*   *drainpipe*
20. *rowan*   *mountain ash*
21. *to shoogle*   *to wobble, shake*
22. *to sort*   *to mend*
23. *to stay*   *to live, reside*
24. *through*   *across*
25. *wee*   *small*

Notes
1. *Ashet* is a loan word from French and is unknown in other varieties of English.
2. *Aye* is known by EngEng speakers mainly from archaic sources, songs or nautical usage, but is never used in normal speech in the south of England. In Scotland it is informal but entirely natural.
3. *Brae* occurs frequently in place and street names, and refers to the slope of the hill, not to the entire hill.
4. EngEng speakers talk of *bramble bushes* or even *brambles* for the bushes on which blackberries grow, but ScotEng (and certain varieties in northern England) use *bramble* also for the fruit itself.
5. *Burn* is neutral in style, but is not used in England. Most EngEng speakers, however, probably know what it means. *Stream* is used in ScotEng in the figurative sense.
6. Places which sell hot food to be taken away and eaten off the premises are known in Scotland as *carry-outs*. (In the south of England they are *take-aways* and in the north *take-outs*. *Carry-out* and *take-out* are also used in North America.)
7. *Dram* is usually used with reference to whisky.
8. *Dreich* is a self-consciously Scottish word, i.e. Scots know that English people do not know it, but it is frequently heard.
9. Both *folk* and *people* are known and used in Scotland and England. *Folk*, however, is much more common and more colloquial in ScotEng: e.g. *They're very nice folk*; *There were a lot of folk there*. In EngEng this type of usage sounds archaic, and *folk* is used mainly as an adjective as in *folk-songs*, *folk-tale*, etc. The ScotEng usage is also found in northern England and in parts of the USA. (Also, the plural *folks* can mean 'parents' or 'family, relatives' in parts of the USA.)
10. *Haar* is particularly common in the east of Scotland and refers to the thick mist that comes in from the sea.
11. Scottish hospitals are often known as *infirmaries*, but *hospital* is also common. (Infirmary is also used in the USA, usually referring to a university medical treatment unit where surgery is not performed.)

12. *Jag* (noun or verb) is frequently used in connection with thorns, injections, etc.
13. *Janitor* occurs in this usage also in NAmEng.
14. *Loch*, meaning 'lake', is familiar to most English speakers around the world, from the names of famous Scottish lakes, e.g. Loch Ness and Loch Lomond. The word is originally from Gaelic.
15. *To mind* has all the meanings in ScotEng that it has in EngEng, but it has the additional meaning, in informal usage especially, of 'to remember' as in *Do you mind when we went to Edinburgh?*
16. *Outwith* is not known in EngEng but can be frequently encountered in newspapers, public notices, etc. in Scotland.
17. *Pinkie* is not known by many EngEng speakers, but is widely used in NAmEng also.
18. The Scottish legal system is separate from that of England and Wales, and many different words are used in legal language, some of them having no counterpart in EngEng. Besides *provost* is ScotEng *procurator fiscal* which corresponds to EngEng *public prosecutor*.
19. *Rone* in ScotEng can refer to either a downward-drawing pipe outside a house or to the horizontal gutterings around the roof. EngEng speakers generally have no idea what this word means.
20. *Rowan* /rɑuən/ is known in England, but there it is normally pronounced /rouən/.
21. *To shoogle, shoogly* are informal but very usual in ScotEng.
22. This usage is known in EngEng, where *to sort* simply means 'to arrange, to classify'.
23. *Stay* has all the usual EngEng meanings in ScotEng, but it also means 'to reside, live' as in *I stay at Portobello*.
24. In discussing east–west or west–east journeys in Scotland itself, speakers often use the word *through*, as in *I'm going through to Glasgow* (from Edinburgh).
25. *Wee* is known to EngEng speakers but is not often used by them. It is extremely common in ScotEng.

One is also likely to encounter a number of phrases and idioms which are specifically Scottish. A few are listed here:

ScotEng	*EngEng*
How are you keeping?	*How are you?*
I doubt he's not coming	*I expect he's not coming*
Away to your bed	*Go to bed*
That's me away	*I'm going now*
I've got the cold	*I've got a cold*
It's for your Christmas	*It's your Christmas present*
I gave her a row	*I scolded her*
He gave me a fright	*He frightened me*
I'm finished it	*I have finished it/I'm finished*
I'll get you home	*I'll take* (accompany) *you home*

Cheerio just now!   *Cheerio* (goodbye) *for now!*
To go the messages   *To go shopping*
The back of nine o'clock   *Soon after nine o'clock*

5.1.6. Scots

As we noted above, Scots, which was essentially a language different from though related to English, was the original standard language of the kingdom of Scotland. However, after the Reformation, and the union of the crowns of England and Scotland, it began to lose much of its status. Then, with the loss of Scottish independence and the merger of the London and Edinburgh parliaments in 1707, Scots lost its independence too, and came to be felt very often to be simply a dialect of English. But literature such as that of Burns—and also of many modern writers—continued to be written in the language, and today there is a strong revival movement. The non-standard dialects of southern and eastern Scotland, especially in rural areas, are still also basically Scots.

Scots is in many linguistic respects radically different from most other varieties used in the English-speaking world, as can be seen from this passage from the journal of the Scots Language Society *Lallans* ('Lallans' means 'Lowlands', and is the name often given to literary Scots):

> *For ane an twintie year* Lallans, *the magazine o the Scots Leid Associe, haes featurt the bestest current writin in Scots, baith in poetry an prose. Writers o aa kynds haes kythed atween its batters. Thay'v shawn the ongaun virr an vitality o Scots as a leevin tung.* Lallans *in its editorial policy haes aye setten heich staundarts for Scots writin.*
>
> *For twenty-one years* Lallans, *the magazine of the Scots Language Association, has featured the best current writing in Scots, both in poetry and prose. Writers of all kinds have appeared between its covers. They've shown the ongoing vigour and vitality of Scots as a living tomgue.* Lallans *in its editorial policy has always set high standards for Scots writing.*

It can be seen that Scots is very distinctive in terms of vocabulary and grammar, as well as pronunciation (and therefore spelling). *Batters* is a specifically Scots word which usually refers specifically to book covers. *Haes* 'has' occurs with plural subjects such as 'writers'. And the form *heich* 'high' indicates the use of the voiceless velar fricative referred to in 5.1.2, where Scots preserves a pronunciation that was lost in most of England in mediaeval times. Pronunciations such as that indicated by the spelling *baith*, corresponding to *both*, even go back to dialect differences in Britain that date to the Old English period. It is probably true to say that the biggest linguistic division of all in English-speaking world is between Scots, on the one hand, and all the other varieties on the other. (More information about Scots, together with recordings, is available in Hughes *et al.*, 2005.)

5.2. English in Ireland

Until the seventeenth century, almost the whole of Ireland was Irish-speaking, with English speakers confined for the most part to a few towns. Native speakers of Irish are now, however, few in number and are confined mainly to rural areas of the south-west, west and north-west, even though Irish is the official language of the Republic and is taught in schools.

The English that was originally spoken in and around Dublin was introduced for the most part from the west and west Midlands of England and still shows signs of this today. English of this sort has spread to cover most of what is today the Republic of Ireland.

The English of the north of Ireland, on the other hand, has its roots in Scotland, particularly the south-west of Scotland, since it was from this region that large numbers of Protestant settlers arrived, from the seventeenth century onwards. (The two main ethnic groups of Northern Ireland, today labelled 'Catholics' and 'Protestants', are thus to a large extent descendants of the original Irish-speakers and Scots-speaking settlers, respectively.) For a while, Scots-speaking areas of the far north were separated from English-speaking areas of the south by entirely Irish-speaking areas, and at the level of rural dialects there is still a fairly sharp line that can be drawn across Northern Ireland dividing heavily Scots-influenced Ulster-Scots varieties in the far north from other less heavily Scots-influenced Mid-Ulster varieties.

In this chapter we use the label NIrEng to refer to the ScotEng-origin varieties spoken in the north of Ireland, i.e. Ulster-Scots and Mid-Ulster English, and the label SIrEng to refer to the EngEng-origin varieties of the south of Ireland. This distinction is *not* coterminous with the political division of the Republic of Ireland and Northern Ireland: some areas of the Republic, e.g. Donegal, speak NIrEng, while some of the southern areas of Northern Ireland speak SIrEng. In recent years a standardized form of Ulster Scots, distinct from the Scots of Lowland Scotland, has achieved some limited official recognition as a language in its own right called Ullans.

5.2.1. NIrEng pronunciation

At the level of educated speech, NIrEng pronunciation differs from that of ScotEng mainly in the following respects (many of which can be heard on the recording):

1. The vowel /e/ of *bay* may be diphthongized to [ei]. Word-finally, however, it is often [ɛ·], and pre-consonantally it may be a diphthong of the type [ɛə]~[iə], e.g. *gate* [giət].
2. /ɒ/ and /ɔ:/ may contrast, but only before /p/, /t/, /k/. Thus, unlike ScotEng, *cot* and *caught* are distinct, but like ScotEng, *awful* and *offal* are homophonous.
3. /au/ is often rather different from its ScotEng counterpart. In NIrEng the vowel of *house* may range from [œʉ], [ɛʉ], [æʉ] to [ɐ̯ə] and even [ɜʊ]. Middle-class NIrEng can have [ɑʉ] or even [ɔʉ].

4. /r/ is usually not a flap but a frictionless continuant. Words such as *bird*, *card* are pronounced very much as in NAmEng.
5. In most NIrEng-speaking areas, /l/ is clear [l].
6. Intervocalic /t/ is not infrequently a voiced flap [ḓ], cf. NAmEng.

The intonation of certain types of NIrEng is also very distinctive and resembles that of south-western Scotland. This can be heard on the recording.

English RP exerts a certain influence on the speech of middle-class Northern Irish speakers.

5.2.2. NIrEng grammar and lexis

Most of the grammatical and lexical features of NIrEng which differentiate it from EngEng are also found in ScotEng and/or SIrEng (see especially 5.1.4. and 5.2.6.). A distinctively NIrEng grammatical feature, however, is the use of *whenever* to refer to a single occasion, as in *Whenever my baby was born, I became depressed* ('When my baby was born. . .'). Northwestern varieties of NIrEng also have positive *anymore* as in USEng (see 4.1.3.(11)).

Where NIrEng lexis differs from EngEng, it is usually the same as ScotEng or SIrEng. Of the vocabulary items cited in 5.1.5. (ScotEng), the following (at least) are also found in NIrEng: *aye, brae, burn, carry-out, folk, jag, janitor, pinkie, shoogle, wee*. The word *loch* also occurs in NIrEng but is spelt *lough*. Of the vocabulary items listed in 5.2.7. (SIrEng), *bold, cog* and *delph* can also be found in NIrEng. Other lexical items not found in EngEng include:

NIrEng	EngEng
to boke	'to vomit'
to gunder	'to shout'
to hoke	'to poke around, to dig into, to rummage'
to skite	'to slap, to splash'
to wither	'to hesitate'
throughother	'untidy, messy'

These words are also known in parts of Scotland.

In NIrEng, *bring* and *take* can be used differently than in EngEng, e.g.:

NIrEng	You bring the children to school, and I'll take them home
EngEng	*You take the children to school, and I'll bring them home*

(This is also true of some varieties of SIrEng and USEng. And in some parts of the west of Scotland, *take* would be used in both clauses of the above sentence, while in some USEng varieties *bring* would be used in both clauses.)

Of the Scottish idioms and phrases listed at the end of 5.1.5., the following (at least) are also used in NIrEng: *I doubt he's not coming, I've got the cold, That's me away, I'll get you home, to go the messages.* Other NIrEng idioms include:

NIrEng	**EngEng**
He gets doing it	*He is allowed to do it*
It would take you to be there early	*You have to be there early*
I'm not at myself	*I'm not feeling very well*
You're well mended	*You're looking better* (after an illness)

5.2.3. SIrEng pronunciation: vowels

The SIrEng vowel system can be presented as follows (Table 5.2) and can be heard on the recording (note that the length distinction typical of RP is also found here, while it is absent from both ScotEng and NIrEng).

The RP vowels /ɜ:/, /ɪə/, /ɛə/, /ʊə/ do not occur, since SIrEng is rhotic (cf. 5.1.1.(1)). Note the rounded vowel [ɔ˦] for /ʌ/.

The following points represent variable pronunciation differences:

1. Words such as *path, dance* may often have /æ/ rather than /ɑ:/ (see 2.1.2.(4)).
2. Words such as *hoarse, mourning* may be pronounced with /ɔ:/ (the same as *horse, morning*), rather than with /ou/.
3. Words such as *nurse* may be /nʊrs/ rather than /nʌrs/ = [nɔ˦ɹs].
4. In some types of Dublin speech, words such as *pair* may be /pʌr/ = [pɔ˦ɹ] rather than /peir/.
5. Words like *book, cook, rook* may have a /u:/ rather than /ʊ/.
6. *Many, any*, etc. may be pronounced /mæni:/ rather than /mɛni:/.
7. Some words which have /ɒ/ in RP may have /ɔ:/ in SIrEng (cf. NAmEng, 3.1.1.(2e)). These words include *dog, doll, cross, lost, often, wrong*.

Table 5.2. SIrEng vowels

/ɪ/	[ɪ]	*bid*
/ɛ/	[ɛ]	*bed*
/æ/	[a]	*bad*
/ɒ/	[ɑ]	*pot*
/ʌ/	[ɔ˦]	*putt, nurse*
/ʊ/	[ʊ]	*put*
/i:/	[i:]	*bee, peer, very*
/ei/	[e:]	*bay, pair*
/ai/	[ɜɪ]	*buy*
/ɔi/	[ɔɪ]	*boy*
/u:/	[ʉ:]	*boot, tour*
/ou/	[o:]	*boat, hoarse*
/au/	[ɜʉ]	*bout*
/ɑ:/	[a:]	*path, calm, bard*
/ɔ:/	[ɑ:]	*paw, talk, port*
/ə/	[ə]	*sofa, wanted, horses*

At the level of uneducated speech the following pronunciations, which may also appear in the informal speech of educated speakers, can be found:

1. *tea, please, sea*, etc. with /ei/ rather than /i:/: e.g. *tea* [tʰeː]. This can also be heard in NIrEng.
2. *old, cold, bold*, etc. with /ɑu/ rather than /ou/: e.g. *old* [ɜʉld]. This feature is also found in NIrEng.
3. a tendency to neutralize the opposition /ai/–/ɔi/ in favour of /ai/: e.g. *oil* /ail/.

5.2.4. SIrEng pronunciation: consonants

1. SIrEng is rhotic. The /r/ is normally a retroflex approximant, as in NAmEng and NIrEng.
2. The contrast between /ʍ/ and /w/ is preserved: *which* /ʍɪtʃ/, *witch* /wɪtʃ/.
3. /l/ is clear [l] in all positions.
4. Final voiceless plosives /p/, /t/, /k/ are released, aspirated, and without glottalization. In the speech of Dublin, there may also be considerable affrication in final position: e.g. *back* [bakx], *top* [tʰɑpɸ].
5. The influence of Irish phonetics and phonology manifests itself in the treatment of the contrasts /t/–/θ/ and /d/–/ð/. In many varieties the contrast is not preserved, with the dentals /t̪/ and /d̪/ being used throughout. In other varieties the contrast may be preserved in ways other than that employed by RP. For example:

	tin	*thin*
RP	[tʰ]	[θ]
SIrEng	[t̪ʰ]	[t̪ʰ]
or	[tʰ]	[t̪ʰ]
or	[tʰ]	[θ]
or	[θ]	[t̪θ]

(The clusters /tr/ and /dr/ are realized as [t̠ɹ] and [d̠ɹ] by nearly all SIrEng speakers: e.g. *drop* [d̠ɹɑpʰ]. This is true also of speakers of NIrEng.)

5.2.5. Stress in SIrEng

Distinctively SIrEng stress placement is found in a few words:

SIrEng	*EngEng*
discípline	*díscipline*
architécture	*árchitecture*

5.2.6. SIrEng grammar

There are a number of grammatical differences between SIrEng and EngEng. Most of the typically SIrEng forms are found only in speech, particularly in colloquial styles. They include:

1. The auxiliary *shall* is relatively rare, as in ScotEng, NIrEng and NAmEng. Instead, *will* is generally used.

2. Progressive verb forms are more frequent and are subject to fewer restrictions than in other varieties of English. For example, they can occur with many stative verbs:

   I'm seeing it very well
   This is belonging to me

3. The simple past tense is used when the sequence of tenses would require the past perfect in other English varieties:

   SIrEng   *If he saw her, he would not have done it*
   Other Eng   *If he had seen her, he would not have done it*

4. An aspectual distinction between habitual and non-habitual actions or states is signalled by placing *do*, inflected for tense and person, before the habitual verb:

Habitual	**Non-habitual (on a single occasion)**
I do be drunk	*I am drunk*
(= I am habitually drunk)	(= I am drunk now)
He does be writing	*He is writing*

5. A calque (loan-translation) from Irish involves the use of the adverb *after* with a progressive where a perfective would be used in other varieties:

   SIrEng   *I'm after seeing him*
   Other Eng   *I have just seen him*

   The perfect is also avoided in other contexts:

SIrEng	**EngEng**
How long are you here?	*How long have you been here?*
Did you have your dinner yet?	*Have you had your dinner yet?*
(cf. NAmEng, ScotEng)	

   This feature of perfect-avoidance is also typical of NIrEng.
6. *Let* can be used with second person imperatives: *let you stay here* (= 'Stay here').
7. Clefting is frequently used and is extended to use with copular verbs, which is not possible in other varieties:

   It was very ill that he looked
   Is it stupid you are?

8. Indirect questions may retain question-inversion and lack a subordinator (*if/whether*):

   SIrEng   *I wonder has he come*
   Other Eng   *I wonder if he has come?*

   This also occurs in NIrEng.

9. *Yes* and *no* tend to be used less frequently than in other varieties. Instead, ellipted verb phrases are used, as in Irish, e.g.:

Are you going?	*I am*
Is it time?	*It is*
Did he come?	*He did not*

10. The conjunction *and* can be used to connect simultaneous events in all English varieties, as in *John sang and Mary played the piano*. In SIrEng it can additionally be used to connect a finite clause with a non-finite clause, and is perhaps best 'translated' into other varieties as 'when, as, while':

SIrEng	*It only struck me and you going out of the door*
EngEng	*It only struck me when you were going out of the door*

5.2.7. SIrEng lexis

SIrEng vocabulary in most cases follows EngEng rather than NAmEng usage. In those respects in which it differs from EngEng, it often resembles ScotEng. In some cases lexical forms not found in other varieties are due to borrowing from Irish, while in other cases they may be due to preservation of archaic forms. Distinctively SIrEng usages include the following:

SIrEng	*EngEng*
bold	'naughty'
to cog	'to cheat'
delph	'crockery'
evening	'afternoon and evening'
foostering	'fuss'
yoke	'gadget, thing'

Note also the distinctively SIrEng directional terms:

back	= westwards, in the West
below	= northwards, in the North
over	= eastwards, in the East
up above	= southwards, in the South

|6|

West Indian English and English-based creoles

The focus of most of this book is on varieties of Standard English, the kind of English written and spoken by educated English speakers in different parts of the world. However, in order to explain how certain forms of Standard English came to have the characteristics that they do, it is helpful to go into some detail about various forms of English and related languages which do not come into this category. In this chapter we deal not only with West Indian English (WIEng) and other forms of Atlantic Ocean English but also with English pidgins and creoles.

6.1. English-based pidgins

Human beings appear to be biologically programmed to learn languages in infancy and early childhood: children up to the age of 5 or 6 learn their native language or languages rapidly, fluently and perfectly, and without any overt tuition. Adolescents and adults, on the other hand, tend to be rather bad language learners and only in very rare instances manage to learn foreign languages so well that they can speak them exactly like native speakers.

Whenever someone other than a small child, then, attempts to learn another language, certain processes which stem from this imperfect learning ability will almost always occur. In particular, in the speech of such adult language learners, the language in question will be, to different degrees, *simplified* and *mixed*. Simplification is, paradoxically, a rather complex notion, but it can best be understood as involving chiefly *regularization* and *loss of redundancy*. Regularization, obviously, means treating irregular forms as if they were regular, such as when a learner of English said *I buyed* rather than *I bought*. Loss of redundancy often involves the omission of grammatical material which is repeated elsewhere or is not absolutely necessary for conveying the message intended, as when a learner of English says *she like* rather than *she likes*. Here, the grammatical category of third-person singular is conveyed only by the pronoun *she* rather than by the pronoun and the -*s* ending on the verb.

Mixing is a term which refers to the way in which language learners introduce elements from their own language into the language they are attempting to learn. For example, a French-speaking learner of English will almost certainly have a French accent in their English and may also use certain French grammatical constructions and idioms.

Typically, moreover, compared to the language of native-speakers, adult learners' language will also be *reduced*. Because they do not know so much of the language, and because they use it for a more restricted range of purposes, they will control fewer words, fewer grammatical constructions and fewer idiomatic and stylistic devices.

When a language experiences such simplification, mixture and reduction, we can say that it has been subjected to the process of *pidginization*. When language learning takes place over an extended period, in a classroom, pidginization will tend to be slight. In other cases, however, if contact with the foreign language is minimal and short-lived, and the language is learned or 'picked up' without formal tuition, then pidginization may be extreme. In certain rather special social situations, it can happen that an extremely simplified, mixed and reduced form of language of this type comes to be very useful as a means of communication between groups of people who have no native language in common. It may then, over time, develop a fixed form with norms that are shared by large numbers of speakers which can subsequently be passed on to and learned by others. Such a language is referred to as a *pidgin*.

A development of this type occurred in West Africa, where, as a result of early European contact, a regularized, Africanized, reduced form of English, acquired initially from limited contacts with sailors and traders, became useful as a *lingua franca* among different groups of the indigenous population. It then eventually crystallized into the pidgin language that we today call West African Pidgin English. To this day, West African Pidgin English is widely used as a trading language along the coast of Africa from Gambia right round to Cameroon and Equatorial Guinea. Compared to English, this language is mixed—there are elements in its pronunciation, grammar and vocabulary which are due to indigenous African languages; it is simplified or regularized—there are fewer grammatical irregularities than in English; and it is reduced—it would not be adequate for all the uses that a native speaker would want to put a language to, which is, however, of no significance, since it has no native speakers. (Pidgin languages, by definition, do not have native speakers; a pidgin which acquires native speakers is called a *creole*—see below.) It would be a mistake, however, to refer to this language as 'broken English': West African Pidgin English is a language in its own right, with norms and grammatical rules that speakers have to learn in order to speak and understand the language correctly.

Other well-known English-based pidgins are found in the South Pacific: Tok Pisin in Papua New Guinea; Bislama in Vanuatu; and Solomon

Islands Pidgin. These three pidgins are closely related, and all are official languages in their respective countries.

An extract from a Papua New Guinea newspaper written in Tok Pisin

Bilong wanem Gavman i mekim olsem? Ating as bilong dispela em Gavman i pret liklik. Sapos Gavman i larim ol plantesin long han bilong ol pipel bai ol plantesin i no inap mekim winmani. Em, as tingting bilong Gavman. Ol i wari tumas long mekim lo samting i save kamapim winmani. Olsem wanem long pipel? Ating yumi mas toktok olsem. Bisnis bilong Gavman em long tingting long pipel. Bisnis bilong Gavman em long tingting long klos, haus na kaikai bilong ol pipel. Olsem na yumi mas senisim pasin bilong ronim ol plantesin. Plantesin i mas sevim ol pipel. I no ol pipel i sevim plantesin.

6.2. English-based creoles

In certain rather exceptional social circumstances, it can happen that a pidgin language acquires an importance over and above its use as a trading language or lingua franca. Indeed, in some cases it can become the most important or even sole language of a community and be passed on to the next generation of children for whom it will be their native language. When a pidgin language takes on a full range of social functions in this way and acquires native speakers, it is known as a *creole*. Like a pidgin, a creole is still, relative to its source language, simplified (regularized) and mixed. It is, however, no longer reduced. Because the language now has to be used for all the purposes a native speaker needs to use a language for, the reduction that took place during pidginization has to be repaired by a process of *expansion*. This expansion process is known technically as *creolization*. During creolization, vocabulary is developed and expanded, grammatical devices and categories are added to, and the language acquires a wide range of styles. Creole languages are thus perfectly normal languages although their histories are interesting and unusual, and are just as adequate means of communication and expression as any other human language.

There are many English-based creoles in the world, and the number is growing: Tok Pisin, Bislama and Solomon Islands Pidgin are all currently going through the creolization process, as is West African Pidgin English, particularly in Nigeria and Cameroon. Probably a majority of English-based creoles, however, are spoken in the Atlantic Ocean area, where they are a result of the slave-trade. As slaves from many different African ethnic groups were assembled on the coast of West Africa and transported to the Americas, they found, in their multilingual situation, that English-based pidgin varieties were a vital means of communication, and in many parts of the Western Hemisphere, creole languages developed as a result of this need.

One country where a number of English-based creoles are spoken is Surinam, in South America. The two most important of the Surinam creole languages are Djuka and Sranan. Sranan is the native language of a large section of the population of Surinam and is also widely used as a lingua franca by Surinamese people who are not native speakers. Here is a short piece of Sranan which illustrates how far the processes of pidginization and creolization have removed this language from its English source:

> *Den ben sabi f'a b'e weri, fu di a b'e wroko tranga, dan te bakadina a b'e kot wan pis presi opo na libasey.*

'They knew how tired he was, because he had worked hard, then in the afternoon he cleared a piece of ground on the river bank.'

It is obvious that many of the words here are derived from English:

den	'them'
ben	'been'
weri	'weary'
fu	'for'
wroko	'work'
tranga	'strong'
dan	'then'
kot	'cut'
wan	'one'
pis	'piece'
presi	'place'
libasey	'riverside'

However, the phonological and grammatical structures of the language are obviously very different from English—*ben*, for example, is a past tense marker that is placed before a verb stem—and mutual intelligibility with English is certainly not possible. Clearly, Sranan, although historically related to English, is now a separate language.

6.3. Decreolization

There are a number of other English-based creoles, however, which have a closer relationship with English. Surinam was a Dutch colony until 1975, and most speakers of Sranan had little or no contact with the English language—if they did learn a European language, it was Dutch. In many other parts of the world, however, speakers of other English-based creoles have had much more contact than Sranan speakers, during the course of the centuries, with speakers of English itself. Where such contact has been considerable, a process of *decreolization* has normally occurred. What this means is that, because English had higher status than the English-based creoles spoken by the exploited, impoverished, powerless and therefore low-status slaves, the creoles were influenced by English and became less different from it. This process of decreolization involved the creole languages undergoing differing amounts of *complication* and *purification*. Complication reintroduced certain irregularities from English, and counteracted the simplification that had occurred during pidginization. And purification removed certain of the elements from African and other languages that had resulted from the mixing that took place during pidginization.

There are many such English-based creoles that resemble English more closely than Sranan does, because their speakers have had closer contact with speakers of English. In the Pacific area, Hawaiian Creole English comes into this category, as does, in Africa, the Krio language spoken in Sierra Leone by the descendants of freed American, Caribbean and British slaves. Most of the partly decreolized creoles of this type, however, are spoken in and around the Caribbean, notably in Jamaica, Belize, Trinidad and Tobago, and Guyana, as well as on the smaller islands of Anguilla, Antigua, Montserrat, Nevis, Saba, St Eustatius, St Kitts and St Maarten, and in the Cayman Islands and the eastern coastal areas and/or offshore islands of Honduras, Nicaragua, Costa Rica, Panama and Colombia. A similar creole, known as Gullah, is also spoken on islands off the coast of South Carolina and Georgia in the United States.

In those West Indian locations where English is the official language (i.e. not in Saba or St Eustatius, where the official language is Dutch, nor in the Central American countries, where it is Spanish), we frequently find a social continuum of language varieties, stretching from Standard English at the top of the social scale to 'deep' creoles at the bottom. There is, in other words, no sharp linguistic division between Creole and English. This is the situation which is found in Jamaica. Jamaican Creole is probably the best described of the Caribbean creoles, and has the vowel system outlined in Table 6.1.

The following features of Jamaican Creole pronunciation can also be noted:

1. There is no distinction between /a/ and /ɔ/, or between /ai/ and /ɔi/. Note, however, that after some initial consonants some pairs of words are still distinct, for example:

cat	/kjat/	*boil*	/bwail/
cot	/kat/	*bile*	/bail/

Table 6.1. Jamaican Creole vowels

/ɪ/	*pit*
/ɛ/	*pet*
/a/	*pat, pot, one, father*
/ʊ/	*put*
/o/	*putt, bird*
/i:/	*bee*
/u:/	*boot*
/a:/	*bard, paw*
/o:/	*board*
/ie/	*bay, peer, pair*
/uo/	*boat, for, port*
/ai/	*buy, boy*
/au/	*bout*

2. Words ending in /aun/ in other forms of English are pronounced with /oŋ/ in Jamaican Creole, e.g. *town* /toŋ/ (the same as *tongue*).
3. Jamaican Creole is non-rhotic.
4. The Jamaican Creole consonantal system does not have the distinctions /t/-/θ/ and /d/-/ð/, with /t/ and /d/ being the only phonemes used from each pair: e.g. *thing* /tɪŋ/; *them* /dɛm/.
5. Consonant clusters are often reduced, both initially and finally, but far more extensively in final position:

scratch	/kratʃ/
strong	/traŋ/
child	/tʃail/

6. Most forms of Jamaican Creole lack /h/:

house	/aus/
hill	/ɪl/

Like Sranan, although not to the same extent, the grammar of Jamaican Creole is at many points very different from that of English. For example, tense and aspect in verbs are signalled by placing particles before the verb stem:

mi guo	'I go'
mi de guo	'I'm going'
mi bin guo	'I went'
mi bin de guo	'I was going'

The lexis of Jamaican Creole, as a result of the mixing process discussed above, contains a number of words of African origin. Perhaps the best known of these is the word *nyam*, which means 'to eat' and which comes from the West African language Fulani.

6.4. Post-creoles and mesolectal varieties

In places like Jamaica where there is a social dialect continuum, with Standard English at the top, an English-based creole at the bottom, and intermediate varieties in between, it is usual to refer to the most standard 'top' varieties as *acrolects*, the intermediate varieties as *mesolects*, and the 'deepest', most creole-type varieties as *basilects*.

The grammar of mesolectal varieties of Jamaican English demonstrates some creole-like features, many of which result initially from the simplification process which occurred during pidginization. (It is important to stress here that the term *simplification* is a purely technical term, as discussed in 6.1., and is not in any sense value-laden—there is absolutely no suggestion that the language variety in question is in any way inadequate or under-developed.)

Grammatical features typical of mesolectal Jamaican varieties include the following:

1. Absence of plurality marking on nouns, if the context or a quantifier makes this clear: e.g. *five book* ('five books').
2. Absence of possessive markers on nouns: *this man brother* ('this man's brother').
3. Absence of 3rd person *-s* on verbs: *He like it* ('He likes it').
4. Absence of the copula in equational sentences and with progressives:

   She very nice ('She is very nice')
   He going home now ('He is going home now')

5. Absence of formally marked passives:

   That thing use a lot ('That thing is used a lot')

6. Absence of tense markers on verbs; instead, tense may be marked by adverbs or periphrastically with *do*:

   He walk home last night
   He did walk home last night } ('He walked home last night')

7. In sentences like *He is easy to annoy*, EngEng interprets the grammatical subject (*he*) of the main verb (*easy*) as the semantic object of the subordinate verb (*annoy*); thus, the sentence can be paraphrased as *It is easy for people to annoy him*. In WI creoles and WIEng the grammatical subject may also be interpreted as the semantic subject of the subordinate verb; thus, a paraphrase could be *It is easy for him to annoy people*, which has a completely different meaning.
8. In WH-word questions, subject–verb inversion may occur:

   What time it is?
   Who this is?
   Why you are leaving?

There are areas of the West Indies where no 'deep' Creoles are spoken but where the English shows certain mesolectal, creole-type features. In Grenada, the Grenadines, St Vincent, Dominica and St Lucia, we can be rather sure that this is because these islands were originally (and still are to a certain extent) French Creole-speaking and have become English-speaking only relatively recently. The English of Barbados, on the other hand, may represent—although this is not accepted by all experts—a language variety in the final stages of the decreolization process. In other words, it was originally an English-based creole which has over the years become so decreolized that it is now obviously English, but with a few creole features remaining. The English varieties spoken by Black speakers in Bermuda, the Bahamas, and the Turks and Caicos Islands, which also show relatively few creole features, may have a similar origin.

It is also believed by most experts that American *Black Vernacular English* (see 3.3.1.3.), the kind of USEng spoken by lower-class Black

Americans and sometimes referred to in the USA as African-American English, has a similar kind of background, i.e. it too may represent a historical English-based creole in the last stages of decreolization. (Related forms of English are also spoken by the descendants of freed American slaves in the West African country of Liberia and in a small area of the Dominican Republic.) Once again, this is clearly a variety of English, but it does share a number of features which are not found in White American dialects with the Caribbean creoles. These features, some of which occur only variably, include the following (compare with (1)–(8) above):

1.   Absence of plurality marking on nouns.
2.   Absence of possessive markers on nouns.
3.   Absence of 3rd person -*s* on verbs.
4.   Absence of the copula.

American Black Vernacular English also retains certain traces of the mixing process, preserving, in particular, a number of words of African origin. In fact, some words of African origin have found their way via American Black English into other English varieties. The most famous of these is *OK*, which almost certainly originated in West African languages such as Mandingo.

The West Indies is the one area of the world where the majority of English speakers are of Black African origin. There are, however, a number of communities of people of White European origin. The White population of many parts of the Bahamas speak varieties of English which are basically of a NAmEng type, but with some West Indian features. Indigenous White speakers in Bermuda (not, in fact, part of the West Indies, but with a number of cultural and historical similarities) speak a variety which is also of this type and which resembles most closely the coastal varieties of USEng Lower Southern (see 3.3.1.1.). The White populations of Saba and of the Cayman Islands, however, speak a variety of English which is clearly Caribbean.

6.5. West Indian Standard English

Standard English with distinctive Caribbean characteristics, as we have already noted, is spoken acrolectally in places such as Jamaica, Trinidad and Guyana by speakers towards the top of the social scale. The accents used vary somewhat from place to place. In Jamaica, while the phonetics of the English of educated speakers is very similar to that used by creole speakers, the phonology is rather different and resembles RP much more closely. In acrolectal varieties, for example, /h/ occurs, and the vowels of *bud* and *bird*, *pat* and *pot*, *peer* and *pair*, *buy* and *boy*, etc. are distinguished. Some non-RP features do occur, however:

1.   The /ʌ/ vowel of *but* retains some lip-rounding.
2.   /æ/ is an open [a].

3. /ei/ and /ou/ are monophthongal [e:] and [o:].
4. Jamaican English is often rhotic, especially in more formal styles.
5. /l/ is clear in all positions, as in IrEng.
6. Final consonant clusters may be reduced:

child	/tʃail/
tact	/tak/
wind	/wɪn/

7. A distinctive characteristic of Caribbean creoles lies in their systems of stress, rhythm and intonation. Unstressed /ə/, for example, is much less likely to occur than in most forms of English:

	Jamaican Creole	**EngEng**
Jamaica	[dʒamieka]	[dʒəmeɪkə]
daughter	[da:ta]	[dɔ:tə]
wonderful	[wandaful]	[wʌndəfət]

This trait carries over into Jamaican English (JamEng) and other Caribbean Englishes, and there is a tendency for them to be 'syllable-timed' in their pronunciation, like French, rather than 'stress-timed', like other varieties of English. This means that each syllable occurs at approximately regular intervals rather than, as in other forms of English such as EngEng or USEng, each *stressed* syllable occurring at approximately regular intervals. This can initially make Caribbean English difficult to understand for those unused to it.

Varieties of English in the West Indies have some lexical items which are not found elsewhere; some of them are found throughout the territory, while others are restricted to particular locations.

Colloquial Jamaican English words which are likely to be encountered and may cause particular difficulty include:

JamEng	**EngEng**
to carry (as in *I'll carry you home*)	'to take, transport'
dread	'terrible, excellent'
dunny	'money'
duppy	'ghost'
facety	'cheeky'
foot	'leg and foot'
ganja	'marijuana'
licks	'a beating'
to look for	'to visit'
to mash up	'to destroy, ruin, break-up' (of a marriage)
peelhead	'a bald-headed person'
a something	'a thing'
to stain	'to taste sour, to be sticky'
tall	'long' (of hair)
vex	'annoyed'

Standard Caribbean English is illustrated on the tape with a speaker from Dominica.

6.6. English-based creoloids

A very different creole-like variety of English is spoken in two different locations in the Pacific Ocean area: Pitcairn Island in the remote eastern Pacific and Norfolk Island to the east of Australia. This fascinating form of English is a result of the mutiny among the seamen on the British Ship *The Bounty*, after which nine British mutineers escaped, in 1790, to hide on Pitcairn, which was uninhabited at the time, together with six Tahitian men and twelve Tahitian women. The language developed by their descendants, which is often referred to as Pitcairnese, shows a number of features due to simplification, together with very considerable mixture, particularly in vocabulary, from Tahitian, a Polynesian language. In 1856, a large number of people from Pitcairn were relocated on Norfolk Island, where their descendants are now outnumbered by more recent settlers from Australia and elsewhere. Those there who are still able to speak Pitcairnese (see further Chapter 7), are all also bilingual in English.

Mixed and somewhat simplified varieties of English are also spoken in two different locations in the South Atlantic. The island of St Helena has a population of about 6,000, of mixed European, African and Asian origin. The very remote island of Tristan da Cunha has a population of about 300, of mainly British but also partly American, Dutch and Italian origin (see further Chapter 7).

Pitcairnese, St Helena English and Tristan English resemble the post-creoles of the West Indian area in that they demonstrate a certain amount of simplification and mixture. Although this is clearly the result of the fact that they have undergone some pidginization, none of these varieties is descended via a creole from a pidgin. They were never subjected to reduction (see 6.1.) and therefore never experienced expansion or creolization. We cannot therefore call them creoles or post-creoles. They are referred to instead as *creoloids*. A creoloid, we can say, is a language variety which has been subject to a certain amount of simplification and mixture, but where a continuous native-speaker tradition has been maintained throughout.

|7|

Lesser-known Englishes

The major native-speaker varieties of English are those that we have already discussed: the forms of English spoken in the United Kingdom, Ireland, the USA, Canada, Australia, New Zealand, South Africa and the Caribbean. There are, however, many other places in the world where there are long-established communities of native English speakers. We mentioned some of them in Chapter 1. Here we give a brief account of these varieties and their histories.

The Channel Islands of Jersey, Guernsey, Herm, Sark and Alderney were, until the 1800s, Norman French-speaking in spite of the fact that they had been under the English and British crown since 1066, as they still are today, though they are not actually part of the United Kingdom but autonomous dependencies. The original local French dialect is now dying out, but the English which has now mostly replaced it has a number of distinctive characteristics which appear to be partly due to the influence of French but also to the dialects of the south-west of England. The accent, at least on Guernsey, is basically of a rhotic (see 2.1.3.) south-west of England type, though it also has some second-language features such as /θ/ and /ð/ being pronounced as /t/ and /d/.

On the other side of the Atlantic, Bermuda, one of the first ever places that English arrived in outside Britain, is a British colony about 550 miles from the east coast of the southern USA. The first English speakers to arrive on this originally uninhabited island were some English Puritans who were shipwrecked there in 1609. In 1612, 60 English settlers were sent to colonize the island, and African slaves were transported there from 1616. About 60 per cent of the population today are of African origin. There are noticeable differences between the speech of Blacks and Whites, the former being more Caribbean in character (see Chapter 6), the latter more like the English of coastal South Carolina (USA).

The Bahamas is an independent British Commonwealth state consisting of about 700 islands to the south-east of Florida, with a population of about 300,500. The islands were originally inhabited by Arawak Indians, but between 1492 and 1508 the Spanish enslaved 40,000 natives, forcing them to work in the mines on Hispaniola (now Haiti and the Dominican Republic), and by the time the English arrived the Bahamas were uninhabited. In the 1640s, Bermuda was suffering from religious disputes, and in 1647 Captain William Sayle, a former governor of Bermuda, decided to find an island where he and other dissident Christians could practise their religion. In 1648, he set sail from London with about 70 settlers (Bermuda Puritans and others from England) for the Bahamas. There were further settlers from Bermuda in 1656, and, after the American Revolution from 1782 onwards, many American Loyalists also arrived, some of them with slaves, from the USA. This doubled the White population and trebled the Black. A minority of the population today are therefore descended from English pioneer settlers and American Loyalist refugees, and the English of these white Bahamians has two main sources: the Bermudan English of the original settlers, and the American English of the Loyalists. There was also some white immigration from the Miskito Coast (see below) when this area was ceded by Britain to Spain in 1786. Most of the population, however, is of African descent. Some black Bahamians are descended from slaves who arrived directly in the Bahamas, whereas others came originally from the American South or the Caribbean. Black Bahamian English is closer to White English than varieties in the Caribbean, but it is much further from white English than the Black Vernacular English of the United States (see Chapter 6).

The nearby Turks and Caicos Islands are a British colony consisting of two small groups of islands between the south-eastern end of the Bahamas and the north shore of the Dominican Republic. The population is about 14,000. The islands were not settled by Europeans until 1678, when Bermudans arrived and set up a salt industry. The Caicos Islands were also settled by Loyalists refugees from the USA after the War of Independence, and, as in the Bahamas, they established cotton plantations employing slaves. In 1799, the islands were annexed by the Bahamas, but in 1848 they were granted a separate charter. After the abolition of slavery in 1843, the plantation owners left the islands, leaving their former slaves in charge. The colony was placed under the control of Jamaica from 1874 till 1959, but became a separate British colony in 1962 when Jamaica became independent. Over 90 per cent of the inhabitants are Black. The speech of the islands is often described as being very close to Bahamian English.

The Miskito Coast is the Caribbean coastal area of Nicaragua and Honduras consisting of a strip of lowland about 40 miles wide and 200 miles long. Columbus visited it in 1502, but there was not much European presence there until the arrival of buccaneers in the 1650s. England established a protectorate over the local Miskito Indians, after whom the region is named, and the area was a British dependency from 1740 to 1786, with the British founding the principal Nicaraguan Miskito Coast city of Bluefields. Spain, Nicaragua and the United States at different times disputed the legitimacy of this dependency, but the issue was settled as far as the Nicaraguan part of the coast was concerned by the occupation by

Spain in 1786, and later by a British–American treaty of 1850. There are about 30,000 native speakers of English in this area of Nicaragua who look to Bluefields as their centre. Most of them are of African origin. Several hundred, however, are Rama Indians. The English is a typically Caribbean variety with many creole features. The anglophone Corn Islands of Nicaragua, Great and Little Corn Island, which lie in the Caribbean about 50 miles offshore from Bluefields and have a population of about 2,500, are also Caribbean-English-speaking.

The Colombian islands of San Andrés and Providencia, with a population of abut 35,000, are in the Caribbean about 110 miles off the coast of Nicaragua and about 400 miles north-west of mainland Colombia. The islands were settled in 1629 by English Puritans, and subsequently also by Jamaican planters and their black slaves. The islands were officially given to Spain in 1786, and they became part of Colombia in 1822, after Colombian independence. Their English is basically also of a Caribbean type.

The English-based but African-influenced creoles, semi-creoles and post-creole continua of the Caribbean have already been described in Chapter 6. It is much less well known, however, that the Lesser Antilles of the eastern Caribbean contain a number of communities of white English-speakers. These communities are in many cases the direct cultural and linguistic descendants of immigrants from the British Isles and thus speakers of an English which, although clearly Caribbean in character, may in some respects show differences from that of black West Indians, especially since residential and social segregation has been maintained in some places for hundreds of years:

1. Of the islands which have significant white populations today, direct white emigration to Barbados began in 1627, with large numbers of the migrants being unemployed or otherwise impoverished people from England. Many of the English who arrived later in the 1650s were prisoners of the English Civil War or transported criminals. Irish immigration was also important.
2. The English-speaking Dutch colony island of Saba was claimed by the Dutch in 1632 but settled by white English-speakers coming, often as escapees from indentured labour, from other islands over a considerable period of time lasting until the 1830s. This isolated white community today forms about half the population of the island.
3. Anguilla has a community of whites who arrived from other islands in the late 1600s, later reinforced by other arrivals (some as a result of shipwreck) from other islands who came around 1800.
4. The Bay Islands are a group of eight small islands about 35 miles off the coast of northern Honduras, of which they are part, in the Caribbean. The islands were first sighted by Columbus in 1502 and were settled in 1642 by English buccaneers. Between 1650 and 1850, Spain, Honduras and England disputed ownership of the islands. The islands were officially annexed to Britain in 1852 but were then given to Honduras in 1859. English-speaking Protestants formed the majority of the

population until about 1900, when Hispanic Hondurans from the mainland began settling, but indigenous English-speakers still form about 85 per cent of the population, which is about 20,000: black, white and mixed. The acrolectal accent (see Chapter 6) is rhotic but of a Caribbean type.

5. The Cayman Islands are a British colony of three major islands in the Caribbean, about 170 miles north-west of Jamaica. The population is about 25,000. About a quarter of the Caymanians are European, mostly of British origin; about one-quarter are descendants of African slaves; and the remainder are of mixed ancestry. The Islands were first sighted by Columbus in 1503. They appear to have been uninhabited, but were known to Carib and/or Arawak Indians. They were subsequently visited by Spanish, English and French ships, and were granted to England in 1670. Most of the settlers were British mariners, buccaneers and shipwrecked passengers, plus land-grant holders from Jamaica, and African slaves. The Cayman Islands were a dependency of Jamaica until 1959, when they became a separate colony. The accent, like that of the Bay Islands, is clearly Caribbean but rhotic.

In Canada, the Îles de la Madeleine are a part of the francophone province of Quebec. They lie in the Gulf of St Lawrence between Prince Edward Island and Newfoundland, 240 km south-east of the Gaspé Peninsula. There are nine main islands with a total land area of 230 km^2. The largest islands are Havre-Aubert (Amherst), Cap aux Meules (Grindstone), Loup (Wolf) and Havre aux Maisons (Alright). The islands were 'discovered' by Jacques Cartier in 1534, although Basque and Breton fishermen had known about them long before that. They acquired a settled population in 1755, when many of the Acadian French colonists of Nova Scotia who were expelled by the British escaped there. The islands were ceded to Britain in 1763 and annexed to Newfoundland, but were made a part of Quebec in 1774. At the end of the 1700s, the population was reinforced by further Acadians who had earlier taken refuge on the French-owned islands of St Pierre and Miquelon, but who now preferred the British monarchy to the French republicans. The population today is about 14,000. About 90 per cent of these, as this history would lead one to suspect, are French-speaking. However, there is a long-standing community of about 1,500 anglophones who are mainly of Scottish and Irish origin and who today live for the most part on Île d'Entrée and La Grosse Île. Their English is of a rural Canadian Maritime type (see 3.4.2.).

If we now turn to the South Atlantic Ocean, we find first the island of St Helena, which is a British colony about 1,200 miles west of Africa, with a population of about 6,000. Originally uninhabited, it was discovered in 1502 by the Portuguese, but the English learnt of it in 1588. It then became a port for ships travelling between Europe and the East, and in 1659, the East India Company took possession of it. By 1673, nearly half the inhabitants were imported slaves. As is well known, Napoleon was kept on the island from 1815 until his death in 1821. The island's population today is largely of mixed British, Asian and African descent, and they are all English-speakers. The English of St Helena, as we saw in Chapter 6, is perhaps best described as a *creoloid*. This means that it resembles the post-creoles of the Caribbean, as described in Chapter 6, in that it demonstrates a certain amount of simplification and admixture: it has, for example, a number of creole-type features such as copula deletion, which is clearly the result of the fact that it has undergone some pidginization. However, it does not appear to have descended from a pidgin via a creole. That is, it was never subject to reduction (see 6.1.) and has therefore never experienced expansion or creolization. We cannot therefore call it a creole or a post-creole, which is why we prefer to refer to it as a *creoloid*. A creoloid, we can say, is a variety which has been subject to a certain amount of simplification and mixture, but where a continuous native-speaker tradition has been maintained throughout.

Tristan da Cunha is a South Atlantic British dependent territory which consists of six small islands about half-way between southern Africa and South America. It is said to be the most remote permanent human settlement in the world, the nearest habitation being St Helena, which is about 1,200 miles away. The originally uninhabited islands were discovered in 1506 by a Portuguese sailor, Tristão da Cunha. A British garrison was stationed on Tristan da Cunha in 1816, as a result of concerns that it might be used as a base for an attempt to rescue Napoleon from St Helena (see above) and the islands were formally claimed for Britain. When the troops left in 1817, three soldiers asked to stay, and during the 1800s they were joined by shipwrecked sailors, a few European settlers and six women from St Helena. By 1886, the population was 97. In 1961, a volcanic eruption threatened to destroy the single settlement, and the inhabitants were evacuated to England. Most of them returned to Tristan in 1963. The English is mainly of England dialect origin but shows some signs of pidginization, though probably not enough to be considered a creoloid.

The Falkland Islands are a British colony in the South Atlantic Ocean about 300 miles east of the South American mainland. There are two main islands, East Falkland and West Falkland, with a population of British origin of about 2,100. In 1690, the English captain John Strong made the first recorded landing on the islands. The islands' first settlement was established in 1764 by the French under de Bougainville, closely followed by a British settlement in 1765. The Spanish purchased the French settlement in 1767, and succeeded in temporarily expelling the British between 1770 and 1771. The British withdrew again in 1774 for financial reasons but without renouncing their claim to sovereignty. The Spanish settlement was in turn withdrawn in 1811. In 1820, the Argentinian government, which had declared its independence from Spain in 1816, proclaimed its sovereignty over the Falklands, but in 1831 an American warship attacked an Argentinian settlement on East Falkland and in 1833 a British force expelled the few remaining Argentinian officials. In 1841, a British governor was appointed for the Falklands, and by 1885 a British community of about 1,800 people had been established on the two islands. The Falklands became a British colony in 1892. In the capital and only town, Port Stanley on East Falkland, a new dialect of English has developed which bears some resemblance to Australian and New Zealand English (see Chapter 2). There does not appear to have been much connection between the Falklands, on the one hand, and Australia and New Zealand, on the other, although sheep-shearers have travelled between the two areas, so the explanation for this similarity may be that all three varieties of English were the result of similar mixtures of varieties from different parts of England (see 1.3.). In rural West Falkland each village apparently still shows dialect connections with the particular part of England from which it was settled.

As we saw in Chapter 6, Pitcairn Island is an isolated British colony, about 1,300 miles south-east of Tahiti in the south Pacific. The main and only inhabited island had a population in 1992 of 52. The island was 'discovered' in 1767 by British navigators, but, though uninhabited, showed signs of previous Polynesian habitation or at least visitation. The modern population, as is well known, is descended from the mutineers on the British ship *HMS Bounty* and their Polynesian Tahitian companions. After a lengthy stay on Tahiti, the crew, led by the first mate, Fletcher Christian, mutinied when their voyage to the West Indies had got only as far as western Polynesia, and they set their captain William Bligh and a number of loyal sailors adrift. They headed back to Tahiti, where they collected a number of local women and a few men, and, fearing discovery by the Royal Navy, set off again. They reached Pitcairn in 1790, where, in the interests of secrecy, they burnt their ship. The island community survived undiscovered until they were found by chance by American whalers in 1808. The population is currently declining as a result of emigration to New Zealand, which maintains responsibility for the colony. A range of varieties of English appear to be open to islanders. The most basilectal (see Chapter 6) of these resembles an English-based creole and has many features of Polynesian origin. There has been some considerable controversy about its exact status but the term 'dual source creoloid' might be appropriate, because it has a similar kind of history to that of St Helena, but can be regarded as being descended from a form of mixture of Tahitian and English.

Norfolk Island is an Australian dependent territory in the south-western Pacific, about 1,000 miles north-east of Sydney. The island has a population of about 2,750. Captain Cook discovered the uninhabited island in 1774. It was claimed by New South Wales (Australia) in 1788 and settled by a small group which included 15 convicts. This was abandoned in 1814, but a new penal colony was established there from 1825 to 1855. In 1856, because of overpopulation, the Pitcairn islanders were removed to Norfolk Island. Not all of them were happy, however, and eventually two separate groups returned to Pitcairn. Norfolk Island's current population includes about one-third who can claim to be the descendants of mutineers, the remainder being descendants of later settlers, mostly from Australia and New Zealand. A strong Polynesian influence, stemming from the Tahitian input into Pitcairn, is still apparent in the culture and customs of the island. The local English of Norfolk Island, which is spoken by only about

25 per cent of the current population, is still rather like that of Pitcairn but less basilectal (see Chapter 6) and less mixed with Tahitian.

As far as Africa is concerned, we have already discussed the English of the Republic of South Africa. There are a number of communities of native English-speakers elsewhere in Africa, however.

1. In Kenya, large-scale settlement by English-speakers began in 1901, with many anglophones coming from South Africa as well as from Britain. Modern European Kenyans, mostly British in origin, are the remnant of that farming population. At the time of independence in 1963, most Europeans emigrated to southern Africa, Europe and elsewhere and most of those who remain today are to be found in the large urban centres of Nairobi and Mombasa. They now constitute much less than 1 per cent of the 30 million population. The English of the settlers resembles that of South Africa (see Chapter 2) to a perhaps surprising extent.

2. Zimbabwe has also had a white, mainly English-speaking, mainly British-origin population since settlers arrived from Botswana in 1890. However, only about a quarter of the white population at the time when Zimbabwe achieved independence from Britain in 1980 were born in Zimbabwe. About 50 per cent had emigrated from Europe, mainly Britain, and about 25 per cent from South Africa. (Today, about 25 per cent of whites living in rural areas are native-speakers of the Dutch-origin South African language Afrikaans rather than English.) There are also Zimbabweans of mixed race, called 'coloureds', who are mainly anglophone. The Zimbabwean English of the native anglophone population resembles South African English very closely. Native English-speakers make up less than 1 per cent of the total population of 11 million.

3. Botswana was a British protectorate from 1885 and has been an independent Commonwealth nation since 1966. White settlement in Botswana, consisting of some Afrikaners and fewer English-speakers, dates from the 1860s and has always been confined to farms in areas bordering South Africa. At its greatest, the white population never totalled more than 3,000. The English of the local population is South African in type.

4. Namibia, which was formerly known as Southwest Africa, was a German colony from the 1880s onwards. In 1915, it came under South African control, and it achieved independence as a member of the Commonwealth in 1990. About 6 per cent of Namibians are of European ancestry, but Afrikaans-speakers constitute about 3.5 per cent and Germans about 1.5 per cent of the population. Anglophones of British origin thus make up only about 0.5 per cent of the total population, although English is the national language. The Namibian English of these native-speakers is again, unsurprisingly, of a South African type.

|8|

Second language varieties of English

English is a language which has more non-native speakers than native speakers. As we saw in Chapter 1, the non-native speakers can be divided into two types. First, there are speakers of English as a Foreign Language (EFL) who learn English as a vehicle of international communication. People in Germany or Japan or Brazil or Morocco who have learnt English will normally expect to use it in interaction with people from countries other than their own. Second, there are speakers of English as a Second Language (ESL). These are to be found in those nations where English is used as an official language, and/or as a language of education, and/or as a means of wider communication within the country, by people who are not native speakers. There are many such countries in the world.

In the Americas, English is an important second language in Puerto Rico, and also has some second-language presence in Panama. In Europe, in addition to the United Kingdom and the Republic of Ireland where English is spoken natively, English has official status in Gibraltar and Malta and is also widely spoken as a second language in Cyprus. In Africa, there are large communities of native speakers of English in Liberia, South Africa, Zimbabwe and Kenya, but there are even larger communities in these countries of second-language speakers. Elsewhere in Africa, English has official status, and is therefore widely used as a second language lingua franca in Gambia, Sierra Leone, Ghana, Nigeria, Cameroon, Namibia, Botswana, Lesotho, Swaziland, Zambia, Malawi and Uganda. It is also extremely widely used in education and for governmental purposes in Tanzania and Kenya.

In the Indian Ocean, Asian, and Pacific Ocean areas, English is an official language in Mauritius, the Seychelles, Pakistan, India, Singapore, Brunei, Hong Kong, the Philippines, Papua New Guinea, the Solomon Islands, Vanuatu, Fiji, Tonga, Western Samoa, American Samoa, the Cook Islands, Tuvalu, Kiribati, Guam and elsewhere in American-administered Micronesia. It is also very widely used as a second language in Malaysia, Bangladesh, Sri Lanka, the Maldives, Nepal and Nauru. (In India and Sri Lanka, there are also Eurasian native speakers of English.)

In many of these areas, English has become or is becoming *indigenized*. This means that these second language varieties of English, as a result of widespread and frequent use, have acquired or are acquiring relatively consistent, fixed local norms of usage which are adhered to by all speakers. These varieties of English may differ, often considerably, from the English of native speakers elsewhere in the world, mainly as a result of influence from local languages. Thus native speakers of English may sometimes have some difficulty in understanding these non-native varieties. This is something of a problem, but it is not clear what should be done about it. If, for example, certain features of West African English (WAfEng) make that variety easier and better than EngEng for West Africans to learn and use, then does it matter that British people find WAfEng difficult to understand? After all, Americans may find ScotEng difficult to understand, but no one would seriously suggest that this is a reason for changing ScotEng. There is, of course, a certain lack of parallel between the ScotEng and the WAfEng cases: (a) the Scots are native speakers; and (b) some West Africans and Indians *believe* that they are speaking EngEng, or at least aim at speaking EngEng.

A particular problem arises in the case of speakers of non-native varieties of English who attempt to get English Language degrees at continental European universities. For example, a West African student's English may be more fluent than that of a Dutch student, but is the WAfEng variety valid or appropriate in the Dutch situation, and, more importantly, should such a student be allowed to teach English in a Dutch school?

There are no easy solutions to such problems. We believe, however, that as long as the differences from EngEng in, for example, an African's or Indian's English do not impair intelligibility greatly, then there is no reason at all to object to that variety being used in native English-speaking areas. Obviously, within Africa or India themselves, the margin for tolerance of differences can be much greater. Equally as important, we believe that native English speakers travelling to areas such as Africa or India should make the effort to improve their comprehension of the non-native variety of English (much as Americans would have to improve their comprehension of ScotEng when travelling in Scotland) rather than argue for a more English-type English in these areas.

We now describe some of these well-established second language varieties of English.

8.1. West African English

WAfEng is spoken by non-native speakers of English in Gambia, Sierra Leone, Liberia, Ghana, Nigeria and Cameroon.

8.1.1. WAfEng pronunciation

The vowel system of WAfEng is typically reduced in comparison to that of most native varieties of English, lacking several vowel contrasts. One type

Table 8.1. WAfEng vowels

/i/	*bid, bee*
/e/	*bay*
/ɛ/	*bed, bird*
/a/	*bad, bard, father, butter*
/ɔ/	*pot, putt, paw, port*
/o/	*boat*
/u/	*boot, put*
/ai/	*buy*
/ɔi/	*boy*
/au/	*bout*

of WAfEng vowel system is given in Table 8.1. Different speakers show different degrees of approximation between this system and that of RP.

The following features of WAfEng can be noted:

1. WAfEng is non-rhotic. Thus *ten* and *turn* are homophonous.
2. RP /ɪə/ and /ɛə/ correspond to /ia/ and /ea/ in WAfEng:

   peer   /pia/
   pair   /pea/

3. Words such as *button, apple* do not have final syllabic consonants as in other varieties of English:

	WAfEng	**RP**
button	/bɔtin/	/bʌtn/
apple	/apul/	/æpl/

4. Words ending in *mb—bomb, climb, plumb*, etc.—may be pronounced with a final /b/. Similarly, words ending in *ng—ring, long, bang*, etc.—may be pronounced with a final /ŋg/.
5. There is a tendency for final consonant clusters to be reduced: *last* /las/, *passed* /pas/.
6. There is a tendency for final voiced consonants to be devoiced: *proud* /praut/, *robe* /rop/.
7. A number of words have stress differences from EngEng:

   congratuláte   *mainténance*
   investigáte   *recogníze*
   madám   *súccess*

8. Contrastive stress is rare. For example, rather than an exchange like:

   Did John go to the store?
   No, Bill went

   one is more likely to find a clefted version for emphasis/focusing:

   No, it was Bill who went

9. WAfEng is typically syllable-timed rather than stress-timed (see 6.5.(7)). This is perhaps the main cause of intelligibility difficulties for native speakers. (Intelligibility difficulties work, of course, in both directions.)

8.1.2. WAfEng grammar

WAfEng varies quite considerably from place to place: some of the forms we list below, for instance, occur in Ghana but not in Nigeria, or *vice versa*. It also varies very much according to the education of the speaker and the formality of the situation. Some of the forms given here are not, therefore, employed by the most educated speakers, or at least not in writing. Where the grammar of WAfEng differs from that of other varieties of English, this is often (but not always) due to influence from indigenous languages. This influence is most marked in less educated and more informal styles.

Typical WAfEng grammatical forms include the following:

1. Omission of articles:

    I am going to cinema

2. Pluralization of non-count nouns:

    I lost all my furnitures
    The damages caused are great

3. The use of resumptive pronouns, not only after focused nouns, as in some colloquial styles of English:

    My brother, he's crazy

    but also in relative clauses in a non-English manner:

    The guests whom I invited them have arrived

4. No distinction between the reflexive pronoun *themselves* and the reciprocal pronoun *each other*:

    The like themselves = 'They like each other'

5. Formation of comparative clauses without using the comparative form of the adjective when it involves *more*:

    It is the youths who are skilful in performing tasks than the adults

6. Absence of infinitival *to* after some verbs:

    They enabled him do it

7. The use of progressive aspect with *have* when expressing a temporary state:

    I am having a cold

8. The use of a universal tag question—*is it?*—regardless of person, tense or main clause auxiliary:

We should leave now, is it?   (EngEng: *'shouldn't we?'*)
She has gone home, is it?   (EngEng: *'hasn't she?'*)

9. A non-English use of *yes* and *no* in answering questions:

Hasn't he come home yet?
(a) *Yes* = 'He *hasn't* come home yet'
(b) *No* = 'He *has* come home'

cf. also:

It may not rain tomorrow
I hope so = 'I hope it will *not* rain'

8.1.3. WAfEng lexis

Many differences in vocabulary between WAfEng and other varieties of English involve extensions or alterations to the semantic or grammatical function of English words. Others reflect usages of equivalent words from indigenous languages, while still others are innovations. The list below gives a few examples by way of illustration. Not all the items are found in all West African countries.

WAfEng	*EngEng*
again	'anymore'
amount	besides EngEng meaning, it can also mean 'money'
balance	'change' (i.e. money returned to a customer)
a been-to	'someone who has "been to" Europe or North America' (slightly derogatory)
to bluff	besides EngEng meaning, it can also mean 'to dress fashionably' or 'to show off'
carpet	'linoleum'
corner	'a bend in the road'
chop bar/canteen	'a restaurant serving indigenous food'
coal pot	'a form of brazier for cooking on'
guy	'an outgoing, self-assured young man'
to hear	besides EngEng meaning, one can also 'hear', i.e. 'understand', a language
hot drink	'alcoholic spirits, liquor'
rice water	'rice porridge'
serviceable	besides EngEng meaning, it can also mean 'willing to serve'
sorry	an expression of sympathy to someone who has just had a mishap (corresponds to similar terms in WAf languages); not very usual as an apology
the steer/steering	'the steering wheel of a vehicle'
to take in	besides EngEng meaning, it can also mean 'to become pregnant'

A very distinctive characteristic of WAfEng vocabulary and grammar is the use of 'high' literary style, i.e. the use of long or Latinate words (*epistle* instead of *letter, purchase* instead of *buy*) and complicated grammatical constructions not only in writing but also in speech. This could be due to several things, including exposure to literary rather than colloquial English and the prestige of the written word.

8.2. East African English

English of a distinctively East African type (EAfEng) is spoken as a second language in Kenya, Tanzania and Uganda. The English spoken by Africans in Malawi, Zambia, Zimbabwe and South Africa is also of a very similar type. Most of the indigenous languages in most of these areas of eastern and southern Africa are members of the Bantu language family, and these have naturally played an important role in influencing the nature of EAfEng.

There are many similarities between EAfEng and WAfEng. Differences include the following:

8.2.1. EAfEng pronunciation

1. There tend to be fewer vowels in EAfEng than in WAfEng (8 as opposed to 10; cf. about 20 in EngEng RP), and the way in which sets of words which are distinct in native forms of English are grouped together differs from that in WAfEng. The vowel system of EAfEng is illustrated in Table 8.2.
2. Many speakers do not distinguish /l/ and /r/.
3. /tʃ/ and /ʃ/ may be merged with /s/, and /dʒ/ and /ʒ/ with /z/.

8.2.2. EAfEng lexis

A number of words from indigenous languages are used by EAfEng speakers even when speaking and writing English. These include the following:

EAfEng	*EngEng*
askari	'policeman'
chai	'tea'

Table 8.2. EAfEng vowels

/i/	*bid, bee*
/e/	*bed, bay*
/a/	*bad, bard, bird, putt, f<u>a</u>ther*
/o/	*pot, boat, paw, port*
/u/	*put, boot*
/ai/	*buy*
/oi/	*boy*
/au/	*bout*

duka	'shop'
kibanda	'black market'
manamba	'labourer'
matatu	'taxi bus'
wananchi	'fellow citizens'

8.3. Indian English

In the South Asian sub-continent, English is widely spoken and written in India, Pakistan, Bangladesh and Sri Lanka. We concentrate here on India, where English is an official language and is used as one of the languages of education and wider communication. There are a number of native speakers of English in India, but these are far outnumbered by those for whom it is an additional language.

Like AfEng, Indian English (IndEng) is beset by the problem of norms. There is no general agreement as to whether the standard should be strictly EngEng or whether IndEng forms (especially in grammar) which are used by the majority of educated speakers and can also be found in newspapers should be accepted in the Indian standard.

8.3.1. IndEng pronunciation

The pronunciation of IndEng varies quite considerably depending on the speaker's native language as well as on his or her educational background and degree of exposure to native English. There are, nevertheless, a number of generalizations which can be made.

1. IndEng tends to have a reduced vowel system *vis à vis* RP (cf. WAfEng above), with some contrasts lacking. Which contrasts these are will depend on the system of the particular native language, but often RP /ɑ:/ and /ɔ:/ both correspond to IndEng /ɑ:/, RP /ɒ/ and /æ/ to IndEng /a/.
2. The RP diphthongs /ei/ and /ou/ tend to be monophthongal /e:/ and /o:/.
3. In southern India, word-initial front vowels tend to receive a preceding /j/ and back vowels a preceding /w/: *eight* /je:t/: *own* /wo:n/.
4. In northern India, word-initial /sk/, /st/ or /sp/ tend to receive a preceding /i/: *speak* /ispi:k/.
5. The English of most educated Indians is non-rhotic.
6. /r/ tends to be a flap [ɾ] or even a retroflex flap [ɽ].
7. In some varieties, /v/ and /w/ are not distinguished; similarly /p/ and /f/; /t/ and /θ/; /d/ and /ð/; /s/ and /ʃ/—depending on the region.
8. The consonants /p/, /t/, /k/ tend to be unaspirated.
9. The alveolar consonants /t/, /d/, /s/, /l/, /z/ tend to be replaced by retroflex consonants /ʈ/, /ɖ/, /ʂ/, /ɭ/, /ʐ/.
10. IndEng differs considerably from other forms of English in stress, rhythm and intonation (as do WAfEng and WIEng). These differences make for difficulties, sometimes very serious indeed, in comprehension on the part of speakers of other English varieties. In particular,

IndEng tends to be syllable-timed rather than stress-timed (see 6.5.(7)). Also, syllables that would be unstressed in other varieties of English receive some stress in IndEng and thus do not have reduced vowels. Suffixes tend to be stressed, and function words which are weak in other varieties of English (*of* /əv/, *to* /tə/, etc.) tend not to be reduced in IndEng.

8.3.2. IndEng morphology and grammar

The following morphological and grammatical features are among those that occur sometimes in the English of even some educated Indians and in English-language newspapers in India:

1. Differences in count noun–mass noun distinctions:

(a) the pluralization of many EngEng mass nouns (especially abstract nouns), e.g.:

aircrafts:	*Many aircrafts have crashed there*
fruits:	*We ate just fruits for lunch*
litters (rubbish):	*Do not throw litters on the street*
furnitures:	*He bought many furnitures*
woods:	*He gathered all the woods*

(b) the use of nouns alone which appear only in partitive phrases in EngEng, e.g.:

alphabets:	*He knows many alphabets already* (= letters of the alphabet)
a chalk:	*Everyone pick up a chalk* (= piece of chalk)
clothes:	*I have bought two clothes today* (= items of clothing)
toasts:	*I'd like two toasts, please* (= pieces/slices of toast)

2. An extended use of compound formation. In EngEng, noun + noun compounds such as *facecloth, teacup* can be made from the construction $noun_1$ + *for* + $noun_2$, becoming $noun_2$ + $noun_1$ (e.g. *cup for tea* becomes *teacup*). IndEng has extended this process to include constructions with other prepositions, notably *of.* Some compounds formed from such phrases are transparent in meaning:

chalk-piece:	'piece of chalk'
key-bunch:	'bunch of keys'
meeting notice:	'notice of a meeting'

while others are ambiguous (where *of* can mean 'containing')

fish tin:	'tin containing fish' (EngEng 'tin for fish')

water bottle: 'bottle containing water'
                   (EngEng 'bottle for water')

Other IndEng compounds consisting of nouns and deverbal nouns include:

age barred   'barred by age'
pindrop silence   'silent enough to hear a pin drop'
schoolgoer   'one who goes to school'

3. The use of nominal rather than participial forms of some words when used as adjectives, e.g.:

colour pencils   (EngEng = *coloured*)
schedule flight   (EngEng = *scheduled*)

4. A difference in use of prepositions in verb–preposition collocations:

(a) no preposition:

IndEng   **EngEng**
to dispense ('do without')   *to dispense with*
to strike ('delete')   *to strike out*

(b) addition of preposition:

to accompany with
to air out (one's views)
to combat against
to fear of
to return back

(c) different preposition:

IndEng   **EngEng**
to be baffled with   *to be baffled by*
to get down (from a vehicle)   *to get off/out*
to pay attention on   *to pay attention to*
to tear off/away   *to tear up*

5. The use of *itself* and *only* to emphasize time or place where EngEng speakers would usually use intonation to provide emphasis:

Can I meet with you tomorrow itself?
We will be required to have our classes here itself
Now only I have understood the problem (= just now)
We arrived today only

6. The use of adverbial *there* for 'dummy' *there*. 'Dummy' *there* in EngEng occurs in subject position with an existential meaning and has reduced pronunciation, while adverbial *there* is not reduced: observe the difference in the two *theres* in *There's* (dummy) *some paper*

over there (adverb). In IndEng, one can hear sentences such as the following:

IndEng   *What do you want to eat? Meat is there, vegetables are there, bread is there*

EngEng   *There is meat, there are vegetables, there is bread*

IndEng   *I'm sure an explanation is there*

EngEng   *I'm sure there is an explanation*

7. Different use of some auxiliaries. The auxiliaries *could* and *would* are often used instead of their present forms *can* and *will* because IndEng speakers feel the past forms are more tentative and thus more polite:

We hope that you could join us
Let's finish now so that we could be there early
The lecture would begin at 2:00
We hope that the Vice-Chancellor would investigate this matter

Also, *could* is used in IndEng where EngEng speakers would use *was able to*:

He could just only finish it before we left
I could do well because I studied diligently

The auxiliary *may* is used to express obligations politely in IndEng:

IndEng   *This furniture may be removed tomorrow*

EngEng   *This furniture is to be removed tomorrow*

IndEng   *These mistakes may please be corrected*

EngEng   *These mistakes should be corrected*

8. There are several differences from EngEng in the usage of tense and aspect in IndEng. They include the following:

(a) the use of the present tense with durational phrases (indicating a period from past to present) where EngEng would require the present perfect (unusual in more educated IndEng):

IndEng   *I am here since two o'clock*

EngEng   *I have been here since two o'clock*

IndEng   *I am reading this book since (for) two hours*

EngEng   *I have been reading this book for two hours*

(b) the use of future forms in temporal and conditional clauses where EngEng would require present tense forms:

IndEng   *When you will arrive, please visit me*

EngEng   *When you arrive, please visit me*

IndEng   *If I will come, I will see you*

EngEng   *If I come, I will see you*

(c) absence of sequence-of-tense constraints

IndEng *When I saw him last week, he told me that he is coming*
EngEng *When I saw him last week, he told me that he was coming*

(d) the use of progressive aspect with habitual action:

IndEng *I am doing it often*
EngEng *I do it often*

with completed action:

IndEng *Where are you coming from?*
EngEng *Where have you come from?*

and with stative verbs:

IndEng *Are you wanting anything?*
EngEng *Do you want anything?*

IndEng *She was having many sarees*
EngEng *She had many sarees*

(e) the use of the perfective aspect instead of the simple past (especially with past-time adverbs):

I have been there ten years ago
We have already finished it last week
Yesterday's lecture has lasted three hours
What had you told them on Friday?
I had given it to you yesterday
We had already informed you of that

9. The absence of subject–verb inversion in direct questions, and the use of such inversion in indirect questions (which is exactly the opposite of EngEng usage):

(a) direct questions with no subject–verb inversion

IndEng *What this is made from?*
EngEng *What is this made from?*

IndEng *Who you have come to see?*
EngEng *Who have you come to see?*

IndEng *He didn't go yesterday?*
EngEng *Didn't he go yesterday?*

(b) indirect questions with inversion

IndEng *I asked him where does he work*
EngEng *I asked him where he works*

IndEng *I wonder where is he*
EngEng *I wonder where he is*

10. The use of a universal, undifferentiated tag question—*isn't it?*—
    regardless of person tense, or main clause auxiliary (see 8.1.2.(8)):

    You are going home soon, isn't it?
    They said they will be here, isn't it?
    We could finish this tomorrow, isn't it?

11. Differences in complement structures with certain verbs, e.g.:

    IndEng   *We are involved to collect poems*
    EngEng   *We are involved in collecting poems*

    IndEng   *She was prevented to go*
    EngEng   *She was prevented from going*

    IndEng   *I would like that you come*
    EngEng   *I would like you to come*

    IndEng   *They want that you should leave*
    EngEng   *They want you to leave*

12. A non-English use of *yes* and *no*, as in WAfEng (see 8.1.2.(9)).

8.3.3. IndEng lexis

One distinctive characteristic of IndEng is that there is substantial lexical
borrowing from Indian languages into English. Some frequently encountered words include the following:

IndEng	**EngEng**
bandh	'a total strike in an area'
crore	'ten million'
dhobi	'washerman' (also found in the English of Singapore and Malaysia)
durzi	'tailor'
to gherao	'to demonstrate against someone by not allowing the person to leave his desk/office'
hartal	'a strike used as a political gesture'
lakh	'one hundred thousand'
lathi	'long heavy stick made of bamboo and bound with iron' (used by the police)
sahib	'sir, master'
swadeshi	'indigenous, native, home-grown'

Other vocabulary differences between EngEng and IndEng are due to
extension or alteration of meaning of EngEng words, retention of archaic
forms or innovations. A brief sample follows:

IndEng	**EngEng**
almirah	'a chest of drawers' (from Portuguese)
appreciable	'appreciated'

as such	'consequently, therefore'
backside	'behind, in back of'
biodata	'curriculum vitae'
co-brother	'wife's sister's husband'
colony	'residential area'
cousin-sister	'female cousin'
eve-teasing	'teasing girls'
furlong	'⅛ of a mile' (archaic in EngEng except in horse-racing)
to half-fry	'to fry (an egg) on one side'
hotel	'restaurant, cafe' (not necessarily with lodgings)
jawan	'soldier'
to be out of station	'to be away from the place where one works'
playback artiste	'professional singer who sings offstage while a performer on stage mimes the words'
police firing	'shooting by police'
ryot	'farmer'
stepney	'a spare wheel; a substitute'
stir	'a demonstration; agitation'
tiffin	'lunch'

8.4. Singaporean English

Singapore is an island nation with a population of roughly 4.3 million, with about a three quarters of the resident population being ethnically Chinese. It was a British colony until 1959. The official languages are English, Malay, Tamil and Mandarin Chinese. Mandarin and English have very few native speakers in Singapore—although these are currently increasing—the majority of the population being native speakers of Hokkien and other varieties of Chinese. The English of Singapore (SingEng), which has many similarities with that of Malaya and other areas of Malayasia, is widely used as a lingua franca within the multilingual society of Singapore, and, not surprisingly, demonstrates a certain amount of influence from Chinese. The type of English described here is that of the most educated segment of the population.

In Chapter 1, we discussed a category of varieties of English which we referred to as 'shift varieties', such as SIrEng. These are varieties which were initially ESL varieties but which have become English as a Native Language (ENL) varieties as a result of large-scale language shift. Interestingly, SingEng now appears to be going through this process. While the vast majority of people in Singapore are still not native speakers of English, an increasing number are. And of course they are native speakers of SingEng, which until recently was an ESL variety only.

8.4.1. The pronunciation of SingEng

The vowel system of SingEng is shown in Table 8.3. Educated SingEng is non-rhotic and has most of the vowel contrasts found in RP. The

Table 8.3. The vowels of SingEng

/i/	*bid*
/e/	*bed*
/ɛ/	*bad*
/a/	*putt*
/ɔ/	*pot*
/u/	*put*
/ə/	*sof<u>a</u>*
/i:/	*bee*
/e:/	*bay*
/ɛ:/	*pair*
/a:/	*bard, father*
/ɔ:/	*paw, port*
/o:/	*boat*
/u:/	*boot*
/ə:/	*bird*
/ai/	*buy*
/oi/	*boy*
/au/	*bout*
/jə/	*peer*
/wə/	*poor*

Less standard speakers have many fewer vowels than this and may merge /i/ and /i:/, /e/ and /ɛ/, /a/ and /a:/, /ɔ/ and /ɔ:/, /u/ and /u:/, /ə/ and /ə:/.

phonetics of the vowels, however, is rather different. Other pronunciation features include the following:

1. Although SingEng is non-rhotic, it generally lacks linking and intrusive /r/ (see 2.1.3.(4)).
2. SingEng is syllable-timed (see 6.5.(7)).
3. Word-final clusters of three or more consonants are often simplified to two, e.g. *next* /neks/, *punched* /pantʃ/. This has grammatical consequences, in that present tense *-s*, past tense *-ed* and plural *-s* may be omitted.
4. Most usually, /əl/ and /ən/ occur rather than syllabic /l/ and /n/ in words like *bottle, button*.
5. Word-final consonants are usually voiceless, so that /b/, /d/, /g/, /dʒ/, /v/, /ð/, /z/ are merged with /p/, /t/, /k/, /tʃ/, /f/, /θ/, /s/, e.g. *knees = niece, leaf = leave*.
6. Word-final stops are usually glottalized and unreleased: e.g. *rope, robe* [ro:pʔ]; *bat, bad* [bɛtʔ]; *pick, pig* [pikʔ]. For some speakers, all word-final consonants can be realized simply as [ʔ]: *pick, pig* [piʔ].
7. /θ/ and /ð/ are often merged with /t/ and /d/, respectively.

8. Post-vocalic /l/ is often vocalized to [ʊ] or lost altogether:

milk   [miʊk]
well   [weʊ]
tall   [tɔ:]

8.4.2. SingEng grammar

1. As in a number of other forms of non-native English, some mass nouns are treated as count nouns: *luggages, chalks, furnitures, etc.*
2. *use to* can be used with present tense meaning to indicate habitual activity:

   I use to go shopping on Mondays   'I usually go shopping on Mondays'

3. *Would* is often used rather than *will*:

   We hope you would come tomorrow

4. Again as in other non-native varieties, *is it?/isn't it?* are used as invariable tags:

   He is going to buy a car, isn't it?

5. Another interrogative tag which is typical of SingEng is *can or not?*:

   She wants to go, can or not?   'Can she go (or not)?'

6. The indefinite article is used less frequently than in native varieties of English:

   He is teacher

8.4.3. Discourse particles

SingEng is characterised by a number of distinctive discourse particles not found in other varieties of English, some of them derived from Chinese, and they are used in functions which in native varieties are signalled by intonation and/or syntactic devices. For example, *lah* is a particle signifying informality, solidarity and emphasis:

   Please lah come to the party   'Please *do* come to the party'

It occurs quite frequently in the locution *'OK lah'*; and it is probably derived from Hokkien and/or Cantonese. Other particles include *ah*, which functions as a topic marker; and *lor*, which signals resignation or frustration.

8.4.4. SingEng lexis

Characteristic SingEng lexis consists in the main of items borrowed from Malay, such as *kampung* 'village', and from Hokkien Chinese; and of English words which have been semantically or grammatically extended.

chope	'to reserve'
koon	'sleep'
makan	'to eat, food'
tolong	'help'
alphabet	'letter' (of the alphabet)
hardwork	'hard work'
take	'to (like to) eat or drink'

8.5. English in the Philippines

The Philippines were a Spanish colony from 1521 until 1898, when they became an American colony. They became an independent nation in 1946. The indigenous languages, of which there are about 90, are members of the Austronesian language family. The official languages are Pilipino (a form of Tagalog) and English.

8.5.1. The pronunciation of PhilEng

1. Unlike most of the non-native varieties of English in the British Commonwealth countries, but like most forms of USEng, Philippino English (PhilEng) is rhotic. Phonetically, /r/ is a flap, and not a continuant, as in USEng.
2. PhilEng is syllable-timed (see 6.5.(7)).
3. The voiced fricatives /z/ and /ʒ/ are generally lacking, being replaced by /s/ and /ʃ/.
4. /θ/ and /ð/ are often merged with /t/ and /d/, respectively.
5. One possible vowel system is illustrated in Table 8.4. Notice the following points:

(a) /ɪ/ and /i/ are generally not distinct: *bit, beat* /bit/
(b) /ʊ/ and /u/ are generally not distinct: *pull, pool* /pul/
(c) /æ/ and /ɑ/ are generally not distinct: *cat, cot* /kɑt/
(d) /ɔ/ and /ou/ are generally not distinct: *caught, coat* /kot/.

Table 8.4. The vowels of PhilEng

/i/	*bid, bee*
/e/	*bay*
/ɛ/	*bed*
/a/	*bad, pot, father*
/ɔ/	*putt*
/o/	*boat, paw*
/u/	*put, boot*
/ai/	*buy*
/oi/	*boy*
/au/	*bout*

8.5.2. PhilEng grammar

1. PhilEng, except in the most careful styles, tends to lack third-person *-s* on present-tense verb forms.
2. The indefinite article is used less frequently than in native varieties of English:

   He is teacher

3. Verbs which in native varieties of English require an object or a complement may occur without one:

   I don't like

4. Pluperfect verb forms may be used where native speakers would expect a present perfect form:

   He had already left   'He has already left'

8.5.3. PhilEng lexis

Characteristically PhilEng lexis includes items borrowed from Spanish as well as from Tagalog and other indigenous languages:

from Spanish:
asalto	'surprise party'
estafa	'fraud'
querida	'girlfriend'

from indigenous languages:
boondock	'mountain'
carabao	'water buffalo'
kundiman	'love song'

Glossary

affricate   consonant characterized by the gradual release of air, after a complete closure.

allophone   a particle realization (pronunciation) of a *phoneme* (vid.).

alveolar   consonant produced by the tip or blade of the tongue touching the alveolar ridge (the ridge behind the upper teeth).

anaphoric   referring back to some previous word(s) or meaning.

apical   manner of articulation of a consonant using the tip of the tongue.

approximant   consonant produced by two articulatory organs approaching each other without causing audible friction.

aspect   the marking on the verb or auxiliary indicating duration or completion of activity: e.g. progressive aspect (*-ing*) and perfective aspect (*have* + tense + participle).

aspirated   manner of articulation of a consonant whereby an audible rush of air accompanies the production of the consonant.

causative   a verb or clause expressing causation.

clefting   the grammatical process of focusing on an item by moving it to the front of its clause and preceding it by *it is/was/etc.*: e.g. *John bought a bicycle* can be clefted as *It was John who bought a bicycle* or *It was a bicycle that John bought.*

collocation   refers to words that habitually co-occur.

complement   in general, all elements of the predicate other than the verb.

continuant   a consonant produced by incomplete closure of the vocal tract.

copula   a stative verb which links or equates the subject and *complement* (vid.), e.g. *be*.

coreferential   refers to two words that have the same reference.

count noun   a noun whose referent is seen as a discrete, countable entity (opposite of *mass noun*, vid.); it can occur with an article and has a plural form.

creole   a *pidgin* language (vid.) which has acquired native speakers.

dark l   an *l* produced with *velarized* articulation (vid.).

deverbal noun   a noun derived from a verb.

diacritic   a mark added to a letter or symbol indicating a change in its usual pronunciation.

ellipsis   the omission of part of a sentence's structure which is recoverable from context.

epistemic   refers to a *modal* (vid.) which asserts that a proposition is known or believed to be true.

existential   refers to the use of *there* (*is*) to express existence (as opposed to location).

flap   manner of articulation (here of *d* and *r*) whereby the tip of the tongue makes a single rapid contact with the *alveolar* ridge.

fricative   consonant produced by two articulatory organs coming close enough together to cause audible friction.

glottalized   manner of articulation whereby the glottis (opening between the vocal cords) is constricted.

homophones   words with the same pronunciation but different meaning.

intervocalic   occurring between two vowels.

lateral   manner of articulation whereby air escapes around the sides of a closure, as in /l/.

lingua franca   a language used as a means of communication by speakers who do not have a native language in common.

mass noun   a noun whose referent is seen as being non-discrete, having no natural bounds (e.g. *air*, *happiness*); it cannot occur with an article and does not have a plural form.

modal   refers to auxiliaries used to express speaker attitudes to the proposition (e.g. obligation, certainty, possibility).

morpheme   minimal unit of meaning, used in the composition of words.

neutralization   the loss of distinction between two *phonemes* in a particular linguistic environment.

palatalized   manner of articulation whereby the blade of the tongue approaches or touches the hard palate.

partitive phrase   a phrase usually of the form noun$_1$ + *of* + noun$_2$ with the approximate meaning 'UNIT of ENTITY': e.g. *loaf of bread*.

periphrastic   using separate words rather than inflections to express some grammatical relationship.

phoneme   minimal distinctive unit of sound (the substitution in a word of one phoneme for another causes a change in meaning).

pidgin   a linguistically simplified, mixed and restricted language used in limited contact situations between people who have no common language.

plosive   consonant characterized by complete closure of the vocal tract followed by the sudden release of air.

quantifier   a word expressing quantity.

resumptive pronoun   a pronoun which marks the place of a noun that has been moved elsewhere in the sentence.

retroflex   manner of articulation whereby the tip of the tongue is curled back behind the *alveolar* ridge.

semi-auxiliary   words which have some properties of auxiliaries and some of verbs.

stative verb   a verb which denotes a state of being, relational process or perceptual process rather than an action.

subordinator   a conjunction which introduces a subordinate, or dependent, clause.

syllabic consonant   a consonant that can occur alone to form a syllable, as /n/ in *button*.

tag question   a question consisting of an auxiliary and pronoun attached to the end of a statement.

velarized   manner of articulation whereby the back of the tongue approaches the velum (soft palate).

voicing   refers to the vibration of the vocal cords: *voiced* sounds are produced with the vocal cords vibrating, while *voiceless* sounds are produced without them vibrating.

For further explication of these and other linguistic terms, the reader is referred to David Crystal's *A Dictionary of Linguistics and Phonetics*, Oxford: Blackwell, 2003, and to Peter Trudgill's *A Glossary of Sociolinguistics*, Edinburgh: Edinburgh University Press, 2003.

Selected references and further reading

The journals *English World Wide* (Amsterdam: Benjamins) and *World Englishes* (Oxford: Pergamon) are highly recommended.

Aitken, A. and McArthur, T. 1979: *Languages of Scotland*. Edinburgh: Chambers.

Alleyne, M.C. 1980: *Comparative Afro-American: An Historical-Comparative Study of English-based Afro-American Dialects of the New World*. Ann Arbor, MI: Karoma.

Bailey, R.W. and Görlach, M. 1982: *English as a World Language*. Ann Arbor, MI: University of Michigan Press.

Bauer, L. 2002. *An Introduction to International Varieties of English*. Edinburgh: Edinburgh University Press.

Baugh, A.C. and Cable, T. 1993: *A History of the English Language*. 4th edition. London: Routledge.

Bell, A. and Holmes, J. (eds) 1990: *New Zealand Ways of Speaking English*. Clevedon: Multilingual Matters.

Carver, C.M. 1987: *American Regional Dialects: A Word Geography*. Ann Arbor, MI: University of Michigan Press.

Cassidy, F. and Le Page, R. 1980: *Dictionary of Jamaican English*. Cambridge: CUP.

Chambers, J.K. 1975: *Canadian English: Origins and Structures*. London: Methuen.

Chambers, J.K. (ed.) 1979: *The Languages of Canada*. Paris: Didier.

Cheshire, J. (ed.) 1991: *English Around the World: Sociolinguistic Perspectives*. Cambridge: CUP.

Chevillet, F. 1991: *Les Variétés de l'Anglais*. Paris: Nathan.

Clarke, S. (ed.) 1993: *Focus on Canada*. Amsterdam: Benjamins.

Cruttenden, A. and Gimson, A.C. 2008: *Gimson's Pronunciation of English*. London: Arnold.

Crystal, D. 1997: *English as a Global Language*. Cambridge: CUP.

Deterding, D. 2007. *Singapore English*. Edinburgh: Edinburgh University Press.

Dillard, J. 1972: *Black English*. New York, NY: Random House.

Dillard, J. 1992: *A History of American English*. London: Longman.

Dziubalska-Kolaczyk, K. and Przedlacka, J. (eds) 2005: *English Pronunciation Models: A Changing Scene*. Berne: Lang.

Edwards, J. (ed.) 1998: *Language in Canada*. Cambridge: CUP.

Foster, B. 1968: *The Changing English Language*. London: Macmillan.

Francis, N. 1958: *The Structure of American English*. New York, NY: Ronald Press.

Gordon, E. and Deverson, T. 1985: *New Zealand English: An Introduction to New Zealand Speech and Usage*. Auckland: Heinemann.

Görlach, M. 1991: *Englishes: Studies in Varieties of English*. Amsterdam: Benjamins.

Gramley, S. and Pätzold, K.-M. 1992: *A Survey of Modern English*. London: Routledge.

Hansen, K., Carls, U. and Lucko, P. 1996: *Die Differenzierung des Englischen in nationale Varianten*. Berlin: Schmidt.

Harris, J., Little, D. and Singleton, D. 1986: *Perspectives on the English Language in Ireland*. Dublin: Trinity College.

Holm, J. (ed.) 1983: *Central American English*. Heidelberg: Groos.

Holm, J. and Shilling, A. 1982: *Dictionary of Bahamian English*. Cold Spring, NY: Lexik House.

Hughes, A., Trudgill, P. and Watt, D. 2005: *English Accents and Dialects: An Introduction to Social and Regional Varieties of British English*. 4th edition. London: Hodder Arnold.

Jenkins, J. 2003. *World Englishes: A Resource Book for Students*. London: Routledge.

Kachru, B. 1982: *Other Tongue: English in Non-Native Contexts*. Cambridge: CUP.

Kortmann, B. and Schneider, E. (eds) 2004a: *A Handbook of Varieties of English: I. Phonology*. Berlin: Mouton de Gruyter.

Kortmann, B. and Schneider, E. (eds) 2004b. *A Handbook of Varieties of English: II. Morphology and Syntax*. Berlin: Mouton de Gruyter.

Kreidler, C.W. 1989: *The Pronunciation of English*. Oxford: Blackwell.

Lanham, L. 1967: *The Pronunciation of South African English*. Cape Town: Balkema.

Lanham, L. and Macdonald, C. 1979: *The Standard in South African English and its Social History*. Heidelberg: Groos.

Le Page, R. and De Camp, D. 1960: *Jamaican Creole*. London: Macmillan.

Mazzon, G. 1992: *L'Inglese di Malta*. Naples: Liguori.

McArthur, T. (ed.) 1992: *The Oxford Companion to the English Language*. Oxford: OUP.

McColl Millar, R. 2007: *Northern and Insular Scots*. Edinburgh: Edinburgh University Press.

McCrum, R., Cran, W. and MacNeil, R. 1986: *The Story of English*. London: Faber and Faber.

Mitchell, A.G. and Delbridge, A. 1965: *The Pronunciation of English in Australia*. Sydney: Angus and Robertson.

Nihalani, P., Tongue, R.K. and Hosali, P. 1979: *Indian and British English: A Handbook of Usage and Pronunciation*. Oxford: OUP.

O'Muirithe, D. (ed.) 1977: *The English Language in Ireland*. Cork: Mercier.

Orkin, M.M. 1970: *Speaking Canadian English*. Toronto: General.

Paddock, H.J. (ed.) 1982: *Languages in Newfoundland and Labrador*. 2nd edition. St Johns: Memorial University.

Platt, J. and Weber, H. 1980: *English in Singapore and Malaysia*. Oxford: OUP.

Platt, J., Weber, H. and Ho, M.L. 1984: *The New Englishes*. London: Routledge & Kegan Paul.

Pride, J. 1982: *New Englishes*. Rowley, MA: Newbury House.

Pyles, T. 1971: *The Origins and Development of the English Language*. 2nd edition. New York, NY: Harcourt Brace Jovanovich.

Ramson, W. 1970: *English Transported*. Canberra: ANU Press.

Rubdy, R. and Saraceni, M. 2006: *English in the World: Global Rules, Global Roles*. London: Continuum.

Schmied, J. 1991: *English in Africa*. London: Longman.

Shuy, R.W. 1967: *Discovering American Dialects*. Champaign, IL: NCTE.

Spencer, J. 1971: *The English Language in West Africa*. London: Longman.

Story, G., Kirwin, W. and Widdowson, J. 1982: *Dictionary of Newfoundland English*. Toronto: University of Toronto Press.

Strang, B.M.H. 1970: *A History of English*. London: Methuen.

Strevens, P. 1972: *British and American English*. London: Collier-Macmillan.

Svejcer, A. 1978: *Standard English in the United States and England*. The Hague: Mouton.

Todd, L. 1984: *Modern Englishes: Pidgins and Creoles*. Oxford: Blackwell.

Tristram, H. (ed.) 1997: *The Celtic Englishes*. Heidelberg: Winter.

Turner, G. 1966: *The English Language in Australia and New Zealand*. Harmondsworth: Longman.

Wells, J.C. 1982: *Accents of English: Vols 1, 2 and 3*. Cambridge: CUP.

Williamson, J. and Burke, V. 1971: *A Various Language*. New York, NY: Holt, Rinehart and Winston.

Index

Phonetic symbols are at the beginning of the index, vowels followed by consonants. Words discussed as examples in the text are entered in italics, e.g. *yes/no*.

/i/ 42, 96, 97, 142
/iː/ 17–18, 22, 34, 49
/ia/ 129
/ɪ/ 17–18, 29, 34, 42, 47, 49, 50, 96, 142
/ɪə/ 29, 37, 44, 52, 129
/e/ 96, 97, 103
/eː/ 133
/ei/ 37, 45, 47, 48, 49, 53, 105, 106, 117
/eɪ/ 23, 49
/ea/ 129
/ɛ/ 10, 29, 47, 48, 49, 50, 51, 96, 105
/ɛi/ 37
/ɛə/ 17, 29, 44, 52, 129
/ɜː/ 30, 44, 52
/ə/ 22, 23, 29, 34, 37, 49, 117
/æ/ 10, 18, 22, 29, 36–7, 42–3, 43–4, 47, 48, 49, 50, 51, 54, 96, 105, 116, 142
/a/ 96, 113, 133
/aː/ 51
/ai/ 10, 47, 48–9, 53, 55, 96, 106, 113
/aiə/ 17
/au/ 96
/ɑ/ 10, 42–3, 44, 48, 49–50, 49–50, 50–1, 52, 142
/ɑː/ 10, 22, 23, 29, 34, 36, 96, 105, 133
/ɑu/ 10, 45, 53, 103, 106
/ɑuə/ 17, 22
/ɒ/ 17, 23, 29, 37, 52, 103
/ʌ/ 18, 29, 37, 49, 50, 96, 105, 116
/ɔ/ 42, 43, 44, 49, 49–50, 52–3, 96, 113, 142
/ɔː/ 16–17, 23, 103, 105
/ɔi/ 96, 113
/ɔə/ 16–17
/ɔu/ 37
/o/ 96
/oː/ 133
/ou/ 17, 29, 37, 43, 45, 47, 49, 49–50, 53, 105, 117, 142
/ʊ/ 10, 17, 18, 23, 29, 30, 38, 50, 105, 141, 142
/ʊə/ 16–17, 37, 44, 52
/u/ 49, 96, 142
/uː/ 10, 17, 18, 105
/b/ 129
/d/ 47, 53, 106, 114, 119, 133, 140, 142
flapped [d] 24, 30, 35, 45, 104
/ð/ 53, 106, 133, 140, 142
/dj/ 23, 35
/dʒ/ 132
/f/ 133
/g/ 38
/h/ 114, 116
/j/ 17, 23, 45, 50, 133
/k/ 34, 97, 106

/l/   38, 104, 106, 117, 132, 133, 140, 141
   velarized   18–19, 23, 29–30, 45, 97
/ɫ/   38
/lj/   23, 45
/n/   140
/p/   34, 97, 106, 133
/r/   10, 11, 19–21, 23, 29, 30, 35, 38, 43, 45, 47, 49–50, 51, 52, 95–6, 97, 104, 106, 117, 129, 132, 133, 139–40, 142 *see also* intrusive /r/; linking /r/; non-rhotic accents; rhotic accents
/s/   132, 133, 142
/ʃ/   23, 50, 132, 133, 142
/t/   10, 19, 23, 30, 34–5, 45, 97, 104, 106, 114, 119, 133, 140, 142
/tj/   23, 35
/tʃ/   34, 132
/θ/   30, 53, 106, 133, 140, 142
/ʍ/   19, 30, 97, 106
/v/   133
/w/   29, 97, 106, 133
/χ/   38, 97
/z/   47, 132, 142
/ʒ/   23, 50, 132, 142
[ʔ]   19, 23, 45, 97

abbreviations
   Australian English (AusEng)   28
   New Zealand English (NZEng)   32
accents, and social status   4, 15–16
acrolects   114, 116–18, 122
adjectives   77, 135
   reduplication   39
adverbs   25, 78–9
   reduplication   39
affixes   61, 78, 78–9
affrication   106
African American English   47–8, 115–16
African Englishes   125, 128–33
African loan words   114
Afrikaans   36, 125
allophones
   dark /l/   18–19, 35
   vowels   34
Anguilla   121
articles   75–6, 130, 141
aspect   *see* tense and aspect
aspiration   34, 38, 97
Australian aboriginal languages   26

Australian English (AusEng)   22–8
   pronunciation   22–4
auxiliaries   2, 24, 62–7, 98, 106

Bahamas, history   119–20
Bantu languages   132
Barbados English   115, 121
basilects   114, 124
Bay Islands   121–2
be   3
Bermudan English   116, 119–20
Bislama   110–11
Black Bahamian English   120
Black Vernacular English   47–8, 115–16
borrowing   *see* loan words
Botswanan English   125
Bounty mutiny   118, 124
breaking   47
bring   104
British English   *see* English English (EngEng)

calques   107
can   63–4
Canadian English (CanEng)   6, 53–5, 79
   and bilingualism   54
   differences from USEng   58
   Îles de la Madeleine   122
   loan words   88
Canadian Raising   53
Caribbean Englishes   113–15, 116–18, 119–22
   pronunciation   10, 113–14
causative verbs   71
Cayman Islands   122
Channel Islands English   119
Chinese loan words   141, 142
clefting   107, 129
collective nouns   25
collocations   71, 135
colloquialisms   *see* slang
Colombia   121
comparative adjectives   77
comparative clauses   130
complement structures   35, 138
complication   112–13
compound verbs   99
conjunctions   70, 108
consonants
   African Englishes   129, 132
   Australian English (AusEng)   24
   East African English (EAfEng)   132

final consonants 117, 129
initial clusters 133
Jamaican Creole 114
New Zealand English (NZEng) 30
North American English
    (NAmEng) 45, 47
Northern Irish English (NIrEng)
    104
Received Pronunciation (RP)
    18–21
Scottish English (ScotEng) 97
South African English (SAfEng)
    34–5
Southern Irish English (SIrEng)
    106
West African English (WAfEng)
    129
West Indian Standard English
    117
contact varieties 11, 13 *see also*
    creoles; pidgins
copular verbs 70, 107, 123
coreference 76–7
Corn Islands 121
cot/caught merger 43, 49, 50, 52,
    53, 96
count nouns 74, 134, 141
creoles 111–16, 117 *see also*
    contact varieties
    definition 110, 111
creoloids 118, 122–3

dare 64–5
dark /l/ 18–19, 23, 35, 45, 97
decide 71
decreolization 112–14
definite article 75–6
derivation *see* word formation
dialects *see also* names of individual
    dialects, e.g. North American
    English (NAmEng); non-rhotic
    accents; rhotic accents
    contact varieties 11, 13
    pronunciation 9–10
    relationships between 9–11
    shift varieties 5, 9, 36–9, 139
    syllable-timed varieties 117, 130,
        134, 140, 142
diphthongs 16–17, 23, 29, 34, 45,
    47, 48–9, 51, 52, 53, 96, 103
discourse particles 141
do 2, 25, 65, 66–7
double-object construction 25, 68–9
durational aspect 136

East African English (EAfEng)
    132–3
Eastern New England English 51–2
ELF varieties (English as a lingua
    franca) 4–5, 8, 33, 127–43
    and education 5–8, 128
emphasis 39, 129, 135
English as a second language *see*
    ELF varieties (English as a
    lingua franca)
English-based pidgins and creoles
    109–16, 117, 118 *see also*
    contact varieties
    definition 110
English English (EngEng) *see also*
    Received Pronunciation (RP)
    Americanization 92–3
    definition 5–6
    grammar 59–82
    lexis 87–93
    morphology 60–2, 72–3
    near-RP accents 17–18
    punctuation 87
    Received Pronunciation (RP)
        15–21
    rhotacism 19–21
    sociolinguistic variation 17, 21
    spelling 83–6
ENL varieties (English as a native
    language) 4, 5–7, *12*
Erse *see* Irish
ESL varieties *see* ELF varieties
    (English as a lingua franca)
Expanding Circle Englishes *see* ELF
    varieties (English as a lingua
    franca)

Falkland Islands 123–4
Filipino English (PhilEng) 142–3
final consonants 117, 129, 140
formal registers 71–2
French, influence on Channel
    Islands English 119
Fulani 114
future tense 136

Gaelic 54, 95
General American English 48–51
General Canadian English 53–4
glottalization 19, 23, 45, 97
grammar
    Australian English (AusEng) 24–5
    differences between NAmEng and
        EngEng 59–82

grammar (*continued*)
  East African English (EAfEng)
    132
  Indian English (IndEng)   134–8
  Jamaican Creole   114
  Jamaican English   114–15
  New Zealand English (NZEng)   31
  Northern Irish English (NIrEng)
    104–5, 107
  Phillipines English (PhilEng)   143
  Scottish English (ScotEng)   98–9
  Singaporean English (SingEng)
    141
  South African English (SAfEng)
    35
  Southern Irish English (SIrEng)
    106–8
  Standard English   2–3
  Welsh English (WEng)   38–9
  West African English (WAfEng)
    130–1
Gullah   113

habitual aspect   107, 137
have   25, 65–6, 98
Hawaiian Creole English   113
'high' literary style   132
higher education, and standard
    English   5–8, 128
hypothetical situations   62, 63, 72

idioms   101–2, 104–5, 104–5
Îles de la Madeleine   122
impersonal constructions   25
inanimate nouns   25
indefinite article   76, 141, 143
indefinite pronoun   76–7
Indian English (IndEng)   133–9
  and education   7
indigenization, definition   128
initial clusters   133
Inner Circle Englishes   *see* ENL
    varieties (English as a native
    language)
intervocalic /t/   10, 23, 30, 35, 45,
    104
intonation   133–4
  Caribbean Englishes   117
  Northern Irish English (NIrEng)
    104
intrusive /r/   20–1, 30, 38, 51, 52
inversion   39, 107, 137–8
Irish (Erse)   54, 103, 107
irregular verbs   60–1

Jamaican Creole   113–14
Jamaican English   114–15, 117

Kenyan English   125
Krio   113

lah   141
language contact   11, 13
language shift   5
length, vowels   96–7
lengthening, consonants   38
Lesser Antilles   121
let   107
lexis   31 *see also* loan words
  Australian English (AusEng)
    25–8
  differences between NAmEng and
    EngEng   87–93
  East African English (EAfEng)
    132–3, 132–3
  Indian English (IndEng)   138–9
  Jamaican Creole   114
  Jamaican English   117
  New Zealand English (NZEng)
    31–2
  Northern Irish English (NIrEng)
    104–5
  Phillipines English (PhilEng)   143
  Scottish English (ScotEng)
    99–102
  Singaporean English (SingEng)
    141–2
  South African English (SAfEng)
    36
  Southern Irish English (SIrEng)
    108
  Welsh English (WEng)   39
  West African English (WAfEng)
    131–2
  West Indian Standard English
    117
like   69
lingua franca varieties of English
    see ELF varieties (English as a
    lingua franca)
linguistic change, and standard
    English   11–13
linking /r/   20, 30, 38, 51, 52
literary style   132
loan words
  Australian English (AusEng)   26,
    27
  Canadian English (CanEng)   88
  English English (EngEng)   92–3

Indian English (IndEng) 138
Jamaican Creole 114
New Zealand English (NZEng)
    31–2
Phillipines English (PhilEng) 143
Singaporean English (SingEng)
    141–2
South African English (SAfEng)
    36
United States English (USEng) 88
Welsh English (WEng) 39
locatives 77, 79

Maori 31–2
Maritime Canadian English 54,
    122
mass nouns 74, 134, 141
may 65
mesolects 114–15
Midland American English 50
Miskito Coast English 120–1
mixing 110, 118
modal auxiliaries 62–5
morphology 60–2, 72–3, 134–5,
    140, 143
must 63–4

Namibian English 125
native language varieties of English
    see ENL varieties (English as a
    native language)
near-RP accents 17–18
need 64–5, 98–9
negation 24–5, 71, 98
  negative concord 2
  too 39
  yes/no 131, 138
New York City English 51–2
New Zealand English (NZEng)
    29–32, 33
Newfoundland Canadian English
    54, 55
Nicaragua 120–1
non-negative *no* 35
non-prevocalic /r/ 11
non-rhotic accents 23, 30, 35, 38,
    47, 51, 52, 114, 129, 133,
    139–40
  definition 20
  Received Pronunciation (RP)
    19–21
Norfolk English 118, 124–5
North American English (NAmEng)
    6–7

differences from RP 42–5, 55–6
grammar 59–82
lexis 87–93
morphology 60–2, 72–3
pronunciation 41–58
punctuation 87
spelling 83–6
Northern Cities Chain Shift 48,
    50–1, 52, 53
Northern Irish English (NIrEng)
    103–5, 106, 107
Northern US English 50–1
noun phrases 72–7
nouns
  collective nouns 25, 73–4
  count/mass nouns 74, 134, 141
  plurals 74–5, 115, 130
  possessives 115
NP deletion 35

object NP deletion 35
official languages 110–11, 113,
    127–8, 133, 139, 142
one (pronoun) 76–7
ought 64
Outer Circle Englishes *see* ELF
    varieties (English as a lingua
    franca)

participles 25
passives 69, 115
past tense 2–3
perfect-avoidance 107
Phillipines English (PhilEng) 142–3
phonetic environment
  effect on consonants 30, 38,
    106, 140, 141
  effect on vowels 17, 18, 29–30,
    49–50, 53, 97
pidgins 109–11 *see also* contact
    varieties
  definition 110
Pitcairnese 118, 124
pluperfect tense 143
plurals 74–5, 115, 130
possessives 77, 115
prepositions 80–2, 135
prestige dialects
  pronunciation 4, 6, 15–21
  Standard English 2
progressive aspect 68, 107, 130,
    137
pronouns 25, 76–7, 130
  reflexives 2–3

pronunciation 128–33
  African Englishes 128–30, 132
  Australian English (AusEng)
    22–4
  Caribbean Englishes 10, 113–14,
    116–17
  differences between NAmEng and
    EngEng 42–5, 55–6
  East African English (EAfEng)
    132
  Indian English (IndEng) 133–4
  Jamaican Creole 113–14
  near-RP accents 17–18
  New Zealand English (NZEng)
    29–30
  North American English
    (NAmEng) 41–58
  Northern Irish English (NIrEng)
    103–4, 106
  Phillipines English (PhilEng) 142
  Received Pronunciation (RP)
    5–6, 15–21
  Scots 102
  Scottish English (ScotEng) 9–10,
    95–7
  Singaporean English (SingEng)
    139–41
  South African English (SAfEng)
    34–5
  Southern Irish English (SIrEng)
    105–6
  and Standard English 4
  Welsh English (WEng) 36–8
  West African English (WAfEng)
    128–30
  West Indian Standard English
    116–17
Providencia 121
punctuation 87
purification 113

question-inversion 107, 137–8
    see also response questions;
    tag questions

Received Pronunciation (RP) 5–6,
    15–21
  differences from NAmEng 42–5,
    55–6
  differences from ScotEng 97
  near-RP accents 17–18
reciprocal pronouns 77, 130
reduced dialects, pidginization 110
reduction, consonants 117

reflexive pronouns 2–3
reflexives 130
regional variation
  Canadian English (CanEng) 53–5
  Southern Hemisphere varieties
    21–2, 30
  United States English (USEng)
    45–53
registers *see also* slang
  definition 4
  formal 71–2
regularization 109–10
relative clauses 130
response questions 35, 66–7
    see also tag questions
resumptive pronouns 130
rhotic accents 30, 43, 44, 45, 47,
    49–50, 95–6, 105–6, 117, 119,
    122, 142
  definition 19–20
rhythm 117, 133–4

San Andrés 121
Scots 95, 102
Scottish English (ScotEng) 95–102
  differences from RP 97
  influence on NIrEng 103, 104–5
  pronunciation 9–10, 95–7
Scottish Gaelic 54, 95
shall-avoidance 31
shall/should 62–3
she 25
shift varieties 5, 9, 36–9, 139
simplification 109–10, 118, 123
Singaporean English (SingEng)
    139–42
slang, Australian English (AusEng)
    28
slave-trade 111
smoothing 17, 23, 34
social status, and pronunciation 4,
    15–16
sociolinguistic variation
  Australian English (AusEng) 22
  Caribbean Englishes 113,
    114–15, 116, 119, 121
  English English (EngEng) 17, 21
  North American English
    (NAmEng) 47–8, 52, 55
  Scottish English (ScotEng) 97
  Southern Hemisphere varieties
    21–2
  Southern Irish English (SIrEng)
    106

Solomon Islands Pidgin   110–11
South African English (SAfEng)
    33–6, 125
Southern Hemisphere varieties
    21–36
  sociolinguistic variation   21–2
Southern Irish English (SIrEng)   5,
    103, 105–8
  influence on CanEng   55
Southern US English   46–8
Southland burr (NZEng)   30
Spanish loan words   143
spelling
  differences between NAmEng and
    EngEng   83–6
  Scots   102
Sranan   112
St Helena English   118, 122–3
Standard English   1–8
  definition   1
  dialects   4–5, 11–13
  in education   5–8, 15–16, 128
  history   1–2, 8–9
  and linguistic change   11–13
  spread of   8–11
  styles   3–4
stative verbs   98, 99, 107, 137
stress   133–4, 140
  Caribbean Englishes   117
  differences between NAmEng and
    EngEng   56–7
  Southern Irish English (SIrEng)
    106
  West African English (WAfEng)
    129–30
styles
  definition   3
  Standard English   3–4
  West African English (WAfEng)
    132
subjunctive   71–2
subordinators   82
suffixes   61, 78, 78–9, 134
Surinam   111–12
syllabic /r/   10
syllable-final /t/   19
syllable-timed varieties   117, 130,
    134, 140, 142

tag questions   25, 38, 131, 138,
    141 *see also* response
    questions
Tagalog loan words   143
Tahitian   118, 124

take   104
tense and aspect
  durational aspect   136
  future tense   136
  habitual aspect   107, 137
  Indian English (IndEng)   136–7
  passive vs. active   69
  past tense   2–3, 114
  perfect-avoidance   107
  perfective aspect   137
  pluperfect   143
  progressive aspect   68, 107, 130,
    137
  simple past vs. present perfect   72
  stative verbs   98, 99, 107, 137
  subjunctive   71–2
  tense markers in creole   114, 115
there   135–6
to [be]-deletion   70, 130
Tok Pisin   110–11
too, as negative   39
triphthongs, smoothing   17
Tristan English   118, 123

United States English (USEng)   6
  Black Vernacular English   47–8,
    115–16
  differences from CanEng   58
  lexis   87–93
  loan words   88
  pronunciation   41–53
  regional variation   45–53
  spelling   83–6
usage
  Australian English (AusEng)   28
  New Zealand English (NZEng)   32
  South African English (SAfEng)
    35
  Welsh English (WEng)   39
use to   64

variation in language *see* regional
    variation; sociolinguistic
    variation
velarized /l/   18–19, 23, 35, 45, 97
verbs
  Australian English (AusEng)
    24–5
  auxiliaries   2, 24, 62–7, 98, 106
  complement structures   138
  compound verbs   99
  copular verbs   70, 107, 123
  differences between NAmEng and
    EngEng   59–72

verbs (*continued*)
double-object construction 25,
68–9
habitual aspect 107
Indian English (IndEng) 136–7,
138
irregular verbs 60–1
Jamaican Creole 114
Phillipines English (PhilEng) 143
progressive aspect 68, 107
Scottish English (ScotEng) 98–9
Southern Irish English (SIrEng)
106–7
Standard English 2–3
stative verbs 98, 99, 107
subjunctive 71–2
VP *do*-substitution 67–8
West African English (WAfEng)
130
vocabulary *see* lexis
vowel systems
African Englishes 128–9, 132
Australian English (AusEng) 22–3
Canadian English (CanEng) 53–4
East African English (EAfEng)
132
Indian English (IndEng) 133
Jamaican Creole 113–14
near-RP accents 17–18
New Zealand English (NZEng)
29–30
North American English
(NAmEng) 41–5, 47, 48–51,
51–4, 55
Northern Cities Chain Shift 48,
50–1, 52, 53
Northern Irish English (NIrEng)
103
Phillipines English (PhilEng) 142
Received Pronunciation (RP)
16–17

Scottish English (ScotEng) 95–7
Scottish Vowel Length Rule 97
Singaporean English (SingEng)
139–40
South African English (SAfEng)
34
Southern Irish English (SIrEng)
105–6
Weak Vowel Merger 22
Welsh English (WEng) 36–8
West African English (WAfEng)
128–9
West Indian Standard English
116–17

want 70–1, 99
-ward(s) 78–9
Weak Vowel Merger 22
Welsh English (WEng) 36–9
Welsh loan words 39
West African English (WAfEng)
110, 111, 128–32
West Indian Standard English
116–18
Western American English 49–50
wh-questions 115
whenever 25, 104
will 38, 98, 106
will/would 62, 141
-wise 78
wonder 71
word formation 61–2, 72–3,
134–5
word order 76, 78

yes/no 131, 138
yet 78, 99

Zimbabwean English 125
Zulu loan words 36